tough plants

tough plants

unkillable plants for every garden

SHARON AMOS

photography by Steve Wooster

A FIREFLY BOOK

Published by Firefly Books Ltd., 2003

U.S. Publisher Cataloging-in-Publication Data
Amos, Sharon.
Tough plants : unkillable plants for every garden /
Sharon Amos.—1st ed.
[144] p. : col. photos. ; cm.
Includes index.
Summary: Guide to over 100 plants guaranteed to
thrive in the most difficult conditions.
ISBN 1-55297-528-2
ISBN 1-55297-526-6 (pbk.)
1. Plants, Ornamental. 2. Plants, Ornamental—
Selection. 3. Gardens—Design.
4. Landscape gardening. I. Title.
635.9/ 5 21   CIP   SB407.A46 2003

National Library of Canada Cataloguing
in Publication Data
Amos, Sharon, 1956–
Tough plants : unkillable plants for every garden
Includes index.
ISBN 1-55297-528-2 (bound)
ISBN 1-55297-526-6 (pbk.)
1. Plants, Ornamental. 2. Plants, Ornamental—Selection.
I. Title.
SB405.A54 2003   635.9   C2001-903299-4

First published in the United States in 2003 by
Firefly Books (U.S.) Inc.
P.O. Box 1338, Ellicot Station
Buffalo, New York 14205

First published in Canada in 2003 by
Firefly Books Ltd.
3680 Victoria Park Avenue
Toronto, Ontario M2H 3K1

Senior Editor Clare Churly
Editor Lydia Darbyshire
Design Ruth Hope
Photography Steve Wooster

Reproduction by Classicscan Pte Limited, Singapore
Printed by Imago Singapore

This book was typeset using
Gill Sans and Fairfield

Contents

Introduction

Most gardens do not have smooth, flat lawns and beds of rich, easily dug soil. We have to put up with damp, sunless corridors between houses, awkward slopes, or plots shaded by trees or neighboring buildings. Equally difficult to plant are seaside gardens, which are exposed to gale-force winds and salt spray; waterlogged plots, where the drainage is poor; and dry ground, which is exposed to the merciless glare of the sun day after day, without the slightest shade. In short, few gardens enjoy perfect conditions.

If you try to plant any of these difficult areas with a standard selection of garden-center plants the chances are that you will end up with an unsightly display of brown leaves and dried stems as the plants are defeated by the unsuitable habitat.

What you need for these sites are tough plants, which will not only shrug off all the worst conditions in your garden but actually thrive in them and grow well. Of course, these plants are not unkillable—put drought-tolerant heather into a bog garden and it will die—but they are practically invincible in the specific hostile conditions they have evolved to withstand.

Above right: Scotch broom (Cytisus scoparius) tolerates poor soil and thrives in an open, sunny site that is baked dry in summer.

Below right: Salt-laden winds are no problem for shrubby hare's ear (Bupleurum fruticosum), making it ideal for seaside gardens.

Far right: Hardy species of hebe put up with sandy soil and the relentless glare of the sun.

Getting to know your soil

Before you start to plant, you need to build an accurate picture of your garden's terrain. It's rare that a garden is uniform throughout. Most gardens have one or two problem areas, such as the dense, dry shade beneath an evergreen tree or perhaps a patch of poor, stony soil where construction rubble has been dumped in the past.

The soil is as good a place as any to begin an assessment of your garden. Scooping up a handful of soil can tell you a lot about it. Sandy soil will run through your fingers and have a gritty feel. In prolonged wet weather, clay soil is heavy and sticky, like a handful of modeling clay, and when all the moisture has gone it becomes rock hard. Chalky soil is pale and stony, while peaty soil is brown and wet—if you compress a handful, you can often squeeze out some water.

Loam is the best of all soils, a mixture of clay, silt, and sand in roughly equal quantities. Loam is brown and crumbly, without being as sticky as clay or as free-draining as sand. If you squeeze it and it holds its shape for a moment and then crumbles, you have loam. Once you get to know your soil, it will help you to choose plants that will thrive in it.

Soil pH

The fertility of soil is also directly related to its pH value. This determines whether the soil is acidic, neutral or alkaline (limy). Ideally, soil should be neutral, or slightly acidic with a pH value of between 6.5 and 7. (Values below 7 are acidic; those above indicate alkaline soil.) Soils that are too acidic or too alkaline prevent plants from taking up vital nutrients. In acidic soils, plants cannot absorb calcium or magnesium efficiently. Neither do they get correct amounts of nitrogen, potassium and phosphorus. It's rather like eating a diet that doesn't contain enough vitamins—the results are stunted growth and deformed leaves.

Very alkaline soils have a similar effect. The nutrients iron and manganese become more firmly attached to soil particles in alkaline conditions, and if plants cannot absorb enough of them, they start to show telltale signs of yellowing leaves.

Garden centers sell kits and slightly more expensive electronic meters so that you can measure your soil's pH. If you use either of these, take a range of samples from around the garden, because pH can vary considerably within a small area.

SOIL CHECKLIST

Soil type	Characteristics	Soil type	Characteristics
Sandy	• Contains little organic material, which means that it tends to be poor in nutrients • Dries out quickly • The gritty, sandy structure makes it free-draining	Loam	• The easiest soil to work • Rich in organic material and therefore in nutrients • Stays moist without becoming waterlogged
Clay	• Is heavy and sticky • Will bake solid and crack in summer • May get waterlogged in wet spells • Is slow to drain and badly aerated	Silt	• Finely grained and fertile • Easily compacted, and once the soil becomes packed down, the air pockets get flattened and the soil drains badly
Peaty	• Acidic • Contains plenty of organic material in a partly rotted state • Wet and may even be waterlogged	Chalky	• Alkaline • Tends to be shallow and studded with stones • Dries out quickly • Generally poor in nutrients

Healthy, vigorous rhododendrons growing in a garden are a sure indication that the soil is acidic. Here, the rhododendrons are underplanted with ferns, which suggests that the soil is also slightly damp.

The evergreen shrub Jerusalem sage (Phlomis fruticosa) is a plant of hot, dry places, so it's a safe bet that this border gets plenty of sun and that the soil is free draining and not too rich.

11

A soil-testing meter has a probe that you push into the soil for an instant reading. Using a soil-testing kit involves mixing a sample of soil with a chemical solution, leaving it to stand, and matching the color it turns against the chart supplied. If the solution turns yellow, your soil is acidic; if it turns bright green, the soil is neutral. Dark green means it is alkaline.

An easier—and instant—way to assess the soil is to look at the plants already growing in your own garden and in your neighbors' gardens. Vigorous, healthy rhododendrons and camellias and beds of heathers indicate an acidic soil, as these species dislike alkaline or limy conditions. Lilac, hawthorn, fuchsias and achillea (yarrow), on the other hand, can point to an alkaline soil.

Even the weeds you find in your garden can give you some general indications about your garden. Yellow rocket (*Barbarea vulgaris*) does well in dry, sunny places, while the dreaded purple loosestrife (*Lythrum salicaria*), a strange, bristly, prehistoric plant, prefers moist soil that doesn't dry out.

USING A SIMPLE SOIL-TESTING KIT

Mix a sample of soil with the chemical solution supplied with the test kit, then assess the resulting color once it has had time to develop—usually after a few minutes.

Your garden's microclimate

Sun and shade

Sunlight plays an essential role in photosynthesis, the process by which leaves turn carbon dioxide and water into sugars to make the plant grow. But the amount of light that different plants need varies enormously, as can the range of light levels that a particular species will tolerate. Some sun-loving plants will still do well in light shade; and it is possible to grow some shade-loving plants in sunnier positions than normal, usually with the proviso that the soil doesn't dry out.

Trees, bushes, buildings, hedges, and fences all cast shade, but rarely do they plunge an area into permanent gloom. You need to walk around the garden at different times of day to see where sunlight and shadows fall. Remember, too, that in winter the sun is much lower in the sky and can reach into more tucked-away corners.

Dappled summer shade from deciduous trees and shrubs can be used to mimic woodland conditions. Evergreen bushes and trees cast a denser shadow, but there are still plants that can cope with that degree of limited light. The darkest areas tend to be found in city gardens, where older houses are close together, creating narrow, shaded corridors. But even these sunless corridors can be brought to life with the right plants.

At the other extreme are open sites away from trees and buildings, which are exposed to full sun throughout the day.

Perhaps the most difficult parts of the garden to plant are those places that catch the early morning sun. On frosty winter and spring mornings a blast of sunshine can thaw frozen buds and leaves too quickly, reducing parts of the plants to a pulp.

Grasses are plants of the open prairie, making them ideal for hot, sunny gardens. They don't like rich soil, which encourages floppy growth, and put on their best performance where the ground is poor and stony.

Shady gardens offer protection from the sun for large-leafed plants. Some variegated shrubs can be damaged by overexposure to sunlight, so they too appreciate a shady corner, while at the same time, their leaves can help brighten up the area.

Wind

Circulating air in a garden is vital for healthy plants. It prevents the build-up of fungal spores and subsequent plant diseases. But you can, of course, have too much of a good thing. Strong winds can cause excessive transpiration in plants, making them lose too much water from the leaf surfaces so that the whole plant wilts and keels over. This effect is particularly noticeable on warm, windy days. Plants usually recover in the cool of the evening, but if they have lost too much water the leaves may show signs of scorching, with blackened edges or dried brown areas. Strong winds also cause permanent damage by snapping fragile stems and by weakening the roots' grip on the soil so that the plant is lifted partly out of the ground. This is called "wind rock."

Some winds are warmer than others, and you will soon work out which they are. If your garden is in an area dominated by strong, cold winds,

you may find scorched leaves on only one side of a plant. On very exposed sites, and particularly in coastal gardens with no windbreaks, shrubs and trees will be shaped by the wind into typical bent forms, bowed away from the direction of the strongest gales.

CHECKLIST

Before you can start to make decisions about which plants to buy and where to plant them, you need to get an overall picture of your garden by investigating the following:

- *Soil type*
- *Soil pH*
- *Shady areas*
- *Sunny areas*
- *Exposed areas*
- *Sheltered areas*

IMPROVING WHAT YOU HAVE

Improving your soil

Although plants should always be chosen to suit the conditions in your garden, there is much that you can do to improve the soil and provide extra protection to give your plants the best possible start.

It would be unrealistic and impracticable to attempt actually to change the nature of your soil, and by choosing tough plants for particular situations, you are working with nature, not against it. But there are plenty of ways to improve what you have got. By enhancing the structure of the soil and increasing its fertility, you can give plants a head start in getting established, and ultimately thriving, in difficult conditions.

Soils can be too wet, too dry, too acidic, too alkaline, or lacking in nutrients. There are strategies for dealing with all these problems, and throughout this section, one "miracle" solution keeps recurring—well-rotted manure or compost. It can improve drainage in one soil, yet increase moisture-retention in another, lower pH values toward neutral, and, of course, add plant nutrients. Never add fresh manure to the soil. When it breaks down it uses up valuable nitrogen, starving the plants it was intended to help.

Making clay soil easier to work with

Raw, uncultivated clay soil needs extra drainage. Digging in horticultural grit or gravel will help. Add at least a bucketful per square yard (meter)

or so and dig it in to the depth of a garden fork or around 10 inches (25 cm). Timing is critical. In winter the ground can be frozen or too wet to dig, but in summer it can be so hard that a garden fork will rebound without making an impression. In spring, as soon as the soil is relatively workable— not too hard and not too sticky—get as much work done as you can. Using a fork rather than a spade makes digging clay easier, and the sharp edge of a spade can flatten precious air pockets in the soil and actually make the drainage worse.

Well-rotted manure and homemade garden compost will improve clay soil by aerating it and helping it drain better. Again, dig it in when the soil is workable.

To reduce the cracking and baking that are typical of clay soil in summer, use a mulch (see page 36). It can be bark or wood chippings or well-rotted manure. Spread the mulch on the soil surface between autumn and spring, but only do it when the soil is wet after a good downpour. Mulching dry soil will slow down the time the rain takes to reach it and make things worse. Similarly, do not mulch frozen soil, or it will take ages to thaw.

Opposite: Once heavy clay has been improved by digging in well-rotted manure and horticultural grit, it becomes an ideal soil for plantain lilies (Hosta), which like moisture-retentive soil.

DIGGING IN HORTICULTURAL GRIT

1 There's no need to measure out a square yard (meter) precisely, just pace out three "feet" in either direction, then spread a bucketful of horticultural grit over the area.

2 Dig in the grit thoroughly, preferably to the depth of the spade you're using. On heavy clay soils, it's better to use a fork rather than a spade to work the grit into the soil.

17

APPLYING CHIPPED BARK MULCH

1 Only apply a mulch after a good downpour, when the ground is properly wet. It can be a good idea to sprinkle a handful of slow-release fertilizer onto the soil surface first.

2 A mulch needs to be at least 2 inches (5 cm) deep to be effective at retaining moisture. Heap it up around plants but do not let it come into contact with the base of stems and leaves, which may start to rot.

Improving sandy and chalky soils

Rainwater washes through both these soils quickly, taking with it vital nutrients before the roots have a chance to absorb them. Adding plenty of well-rotted manure or garden compost acts in two ways to improve the soil: it bulks up the soil structure, and it provides extra nutrients.

Chalky soil tends to be alkaline. Adding organic materials such as manure and compost, which are naturally acidic, can lower the soil's pH toward neutral, allowing you to grow a greater range of plants. Every time you dig chalky soil, pick out as many stones as you can to give roots room to grow without obstruction.

Both soil types benefit from mulching to conserve moisture. Well-rotted garden compost, bark chippings, or even a thick layer of gravel will all help to prevent precious water evaporating from the surface of the soil.

Many primulas, especially the species that grow in bogs or permanently damp areas, enjoy the acidic conditions of marshy, peat-based soil. Even border primulas appreciate moisture-retentive soil enriched with acidic leaf mold.

Working with acidic soil

A wide range of plants—rhododendrons, camellias and some heathers, for example—will simply not grow in any other soil but acidic. But soil can be too acidic at the lower end of the scale, and the pH can be increased to adding garden lime to bring the pH to a more workable level. The recommended time to do this is in winter: scatter about 7 ounces (120 g) of lime per square yard (meter) and leave it to be washed into the soil with the rain. The effect is not instant and is fairly temporary, too, and will have

ADDING LIME

Wear gloves when working with lime and choose a calm day so that it isn't blown around. Scatter it on the surface at a rate of 7 ounces (120 g) per square yard (meter).

to be repeated every few years. Do not be tempted to sprinkle on a little more "for luck"— too much lime will affect the nutrients available in the soil just as adversely as over-acidity.

Improving peaty soil

Peaty soil is naturally acidic because it consists largely of decomposed grasses and mosses, but it may be too low in nutrients for even typical acid-loving plants, such as rhododendrons. Once again, adding well-rotted manure or garden compost to the soil is the solution, even though it may seem contradictory to be adding more acidic organic matter. The main advantage of digging in some manure or compost is that it adds nutrients. At the same time, it improves the drainage in peat by opening up the soil structure. This goes some way to prevent the waterlogging to which peat is prone.

Dealing with waterlogged soil

If you have soil that stays permanently wet all year-round there is a whole category of exotic-looking species that you can grow. But even water-loving plants need a degree of drainage— stagnant water will not only rot the roots, but will

STABILIZING A BARE SLOPE

The topsoil of a newly created bank or slope is vulnerable. On dry days the wind can simply blow off the surface soil in a cloud of dust, while heavy rain will wash it away. What it needs is a network of specialized plants to hold the surface together and to create a stable environment for other plants to grow in.

Plants that form a flat rosette of leaves are ideal. The leaves radiate from the center and protect the surrounding earth from wind and rain. Verbascums, globe thistles and sea lavender all grow from a basal rosette. Once they have done their job and stabilized the soil, some of them can be divided and moved to create space for other plants.

Mat-forming plants protect the soil, too, but are more difficult to plant into later on, as you need to cut away part of the plant to form a planting space. Nevertheless, they are still worth using and you may find you like the look of a bank and decide to keep it that way.

Rosette- and mat-forming plants protect a bare slope— choosing succulents with this habit is an even better idea as they thrive without special attention.

also smell horrible and be the perfect breeding ground for mosquitoes and other pests. Digging in well-rotted manure or garden compost will improve drainage by opening up air spaces that allow water to pass through.

If water seems to lie on the surface in just one spot after rain, the soil might have become compacted. This can happen where you have had a dumpster in the garden or where heavy machinery has been working. Sometimes all you need do to solve this problem is to break up the compacted soil with a garden fork, to let the water drain away to lower levels. This is definitely not the right spot to spend time and money making a bog garden or damp border because the soil is not permanently moist.

Left: Rodgersia pinnata is a true moisture-loving species and needs soil that is always moist. Don't make the mistake of planting it in a spot that is only temporarily damp, perhaps after heavy rain, but dries out in summer.

Creating shelter

Making a windbreak

Creating some shelter in an exposed garden will make an enormous difference to the range of plants you can grow, and they will be healthier and more vigorous.

Although it may seem like the ideal solution, surrounding a garden with brick walls or solid fences isn't the answer. In fact, it can make things worse. When a strong wind hits a solid barrier, far from slowing down, it actually picks up speed. On the supposedly sheltered side of the wall or fence, it whirls and eddies and can do just as much damage to plants as the full, unfettered force of the wind.

What is needed instead is a permeable windbreak that filters the wind and slows it down without any unwanted side-effects. A windbreak can be anything from a length of garden netting temporarily stretched between two canes to a

Attractive as it is, this wooden fence could actually cause more problems than it solves if intended as a windbreak in an exposed site. Solid fences tend to create turbulence rather than shelter on the side they are supposed to be protecting.

Despite appearances, trellis and openwork fences do a far better job than solid barriers. An open structure filters the wind and considerably reduces its impact on plants in its shelter.

HEDGES

Hedges make good windbreaks if you have the space: an informal hedge of native bushes can be at least 6 feet (2 m) thick, and a clipped hedge only slightly less. However, if you are restricted in what you can grow, the sacrifice of space can be well worth it. On exposed sites choose the toughest species—hawthorn, blackthorn, sea buckthorn—that can survive gales of 60 miles an hour (96 kph) or searing, salt-laden sea winds. As your hedge will be doing such an important job, treat it well. Prune it at least twice a year: exactly when will depend on the species you have planted. Evergreens like laurel and leylandii can be cut back in spring and autumn; box (shown below) and privet can be trimmed more regularly throughout the summer for a really neat appearance. Even informal natural hedges benefit from a light trim from time to time to keep them growing strongly.

permanently planted hedge. "Open" slatted fencing, a chainlink fence or a trellis-and-post system are other options.

Research has shown that a windbreak 5 feet (1.5 m) high can shelter land to a distance of 100 feet (30 m) away. The shelter will create what is often known as a microclimate, a small area with a protected environment within the harsher general climate, and plants growing in this protected area will grow more vigorously, and flower for longer, too.

When you are planting a hedge from scratch, the small bushes themselves will need some temporary protection until their roots are firmly established. Putting up some trellising, chainlink, or temporary fencing for a couple of years will give them a good start.

Beware of frost pockets

When making a windbreak on a sloping site take care that you do not create a frost pocket at the same time. A windbreak can trap cold air and stop it from rolling down a slope or hill. To maintain free passage of air, clear out the bottom of a hedge regularly and make sure that open fencing has space at the base for air to circulate.

Weed control

Weeds compete with garden plants for food and light—and they are efficient. When you are gardening against the odds, it's worth getting rid of every obstacle that stands in the way of successfully establishing healthy plants.

Get to know your weeds

Different weeds have different methods of spreading, so it pays to get to know the weeds before you decide how to tackle them.

Pernicious perennials, such as goutweed, can regrow from the smallest scrap of root left in the ground, so you must be fanatically careful and eagle-eyed when digging them out. Loosen the soil with a fork and gently pull the weeds from the base. If you feel any resistance, stop tugging and loosen the soil still further to minimize the risk of leaving fragments of roots in the ground.

Dandelions are deep rooted and will sprout each year from the same taproot. You need to dig right down to pull the entire root out as they will regrow from small pieces left behind. They can usually be hand-weeded using a weeding tool—any tool with two-prongs—the prongs are slid in on both sides of the plant and used to lever it up.

Dandelions, stinging nettles, creeping meadow buttercup, fireherb, and chickweed all reproduce prolifically by seed, so try to deal with weeds before they flower. Even so, there will still be those that escape or blow in from neighboring gardens. When weeds are still at the small seedling stage they can be kept down by hoeing them off regularly and leaving them on the soil surface to shrivel and die. This method works best in dry weather. If the soil is damp, rake them up or they may simply re-root where they are lying.

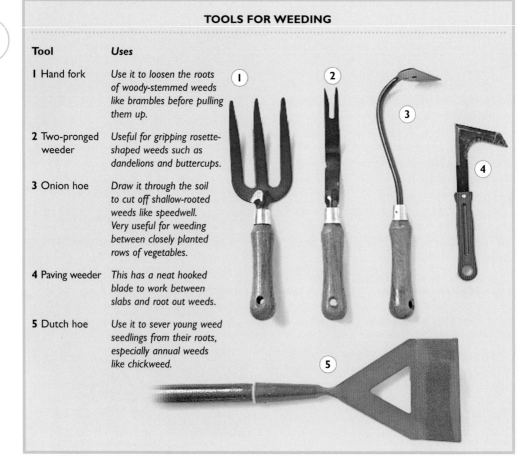

TOOLS FOR WEEDING

Tool	Uses
1 Hand fork	Use it to loosen the roots of woody-stemmed weeds like brambles before pulling them up.
2 Two-pronged weeder	Useful for gripping rosette-shaped weeds such as dandelions and buttercups.
3 Onion hoe	Draw it through the soil to cut off shallow-rooted weeds like speedwell. Very useful for weeding between closely planted rows of vegetables.
4 Paving weeder	This has a neat hooked blade to work between slabs and root out weeds.
5 Dutch hoe	Use it to sever young weed seedlings from their roots, especially annual weeds like chickweed.

USING A TWO-PRONGED WEEDER

Slide the two prongs carefully on either side of the base of the plant where it joins the root. Loosen the plant by shaking from side to side. Then pull. Do not put the roots of perennial weeds on your compost heap.

USING A DUTCH HOE

Use a Dutch hoe on a dry sunny day to slice through annual weeds at the base, then leave them to shrivel. In rainy weather, it is best to rake weeds rather than run the risk of them re-rooting.

23

Clearing the ground

Where a garden is heavily overgrown with weeds, patience is called for. It is best to delay planting for a year and to smother the weeds with an impenetrable barrier mulch to a depth of at least 2 inches (5 cm). Old carpet, black plastic, cardboard, newspaper, a thick layer of leaves, or straw—there are all sorts of inventive ways to block out the light.

You can disguise a less-than-lovely barrier mulch, such as black plastic, by adding a layer of chipped bark over the top of the plastic. It won't contribute to the mulch in any way, but it does look a lot better.

Be careful if you plan to compost weeds. Avoid adding weeds that have gone to seed to the compost heap as it may not heat up sufficiently to kill the seeds. Similarly, many weeds' roots are likely to survive the composting process and to recolonize the soil when you use the compost. It is safer to compost only sappy young green leaves and stems. Alternatively, tie up the worst weeds in a black plastic bag and leave them out in the full sun for some weeks, or soak them in a bucket of water for a similar time before adding them to the compost heap.

Or, to be absolutely sure of disposal, have a bonfire and burn the worst of the weeds.

Deciding when to use chemicals

There may come a point when you are defeated by the tenacity of weeds like bindweed. Then it could be time to consider using a chemical weedkiller. Lots of eminent gardeners do it, and these days there are specific chemicals that target weeds and break down quickly into harmless compounds in the soil.

Patience and repeat applications are usually necessary. A systemic weedkiller like glyphosate is most often recommended for problem weeds. The chemical is applied to the leaves and absorbed and carried around the rest of the plant, eventually killing it. It can help to crush weed foliage underfoot first, before applying the chemical, to aid absorption.

Using weedkiller when weeds are growing vigorously can help it to act faster. Keep an eye on the weather as well: rain can wash away chemicals before they have time to work. When using chemicals, always wear rubber gloves and old clothing, and follow manufacturers' instructions.

Making your own compost

You can never have too much well-rotted garden compost. Dig it into the ground as a soil improver, add a handful to planting holes to help new plants settle in, and spread it thickly as a mulch.

Every gardener has favorite tips for making compost, some secret and some not so secret. There is so much written about it and endless information from experts available in magazines and books and on the Internet. You can even take compost-making courses. But there are a few basic principles to follow that should ensure some measure of success.

Good composting

The best compost comes from keeping a balance between wet and dry ingredients. Whether you build a compost pile or use a manufactured composter, the principles are the same. Build up a heap in layers, using absorbent paper, cardboard, and even old rags between layers of wet kitchen scraps, grass cuttings, and green, sappy plant cuttings.

Build your heap directly on the ground so that worms and soil organisms can get to work on it. A base layer of twigs or a couple of shallow channels dug into the ground will ensure that air can still circulate throughout the heap. Between additions, cover it with a piece of old carpet or black plastic to keep the warmth in. Once the heap is several feet (a meter) high or as tall as you can manage comfortably, weight the cover down with bricks and leave it for a year.

For a homemade composter, use an old garbage can with the bottom knocked out and some holes drilled in the sides for air circulation. This is a neater way of making compost in a small garden. If you have plenty of space, tie together some old pallets or door panels to make two square heaps side by side. That way you can have one heap under cover, working its magic while you are building up the next one. Manufactured composters, usually of heavy plastic, work on the same principles. Remember to turn the compost frequently, and keep the lid on tight to keep out rodents, who will gladly nest in the warm pile.

Invest in a worm composter to deal with all the kitchen waste that you can't add to a compost heap (see opposite). There are plenty of

MAKING A COMPOST HEAP

1 If you have space, make two heaps. Use a series of boards that slot into the sides, adding them as the heap gets higher. The heap on the right has rotted down and the resulting compost is being used in the garden.

2 Cover the compost heap with plastic sheeting or with a piece of old carpet to keep in the warmth and help the composting process.

3 You will know when your compost is ready, because well-rotted compost is rich, brown and crumbly and bears no resemblance to the mixture of materials that went into the original heap.

WHAT TO ADD TO YOUR COMPOST HEAP

You can add almost any organic material to a compost heap:

- *Raw vegetable and fruit scraps*
- *Eggshells*
- *Teabags*
- *Coffee grounds*
- *Some weeds (see page 23)*

- *Crumpled newspaper*
- *Strips of thin cardboard*
- *Paper towels and tissues*
- *Torn up rags in natural fibers (cotton or wool, for example)*

WHAT NOT TO ADD

◦ *Meat or fish (you will attract rats)* ◦ *Bones* ◦ *Fats* ◦ *Oil* ◦ *Scraps of cooked food*
◦ *Diseased plant material* ◦ *Some weeds (see page 23)*

kits on the market, and these are supplied complete with red wiggler worms, which will turn waste food into rich, nutritious worm castings for spreading on your garden.

Leaves rot by a different process. Make a special heap for them alone and leave them for two years to make your own leaf mold. Twigs take ages to rot and make finished compost awkward to spread or dig into soil. They are useful only as a base layer to allow air into the heap. If you have got a shredder, chip them to make a mulch.

Unless you've got one of those compost bin kits that comes disguised as a beehive, even the neatest of compost heaps is not that attractive to look at. If you have space, screen off a small area of your garden with hedging, or trellis and climbers, and site your compost heaps there.

It's a good idea to pave the area behind the hedge or screen. With heavy regular use, grass soon gets trampled into mud in winter, especially if you are trundling a wheelbarrow back and forth, for example.

Choosing the right plants for your garden

Working with nature is the easiest way to plant a garden. Even a small garden has shady corners and sunny ones. On larger sites there's every likelihood that you will find patches of dry soil and damp areas, slopes, ditches, or poor stony soil. There's far less risk of failure if you match plants to these different habitats, because they have evolved over thousands of years to cope with them. Once you have become familiar with some of the ways in which plants have evolved to deal with different conditions, you may even be able to assess an unfamiliar plant and make a reasonable guess where it will be happiest in your garden.

Plants that thrive in hot, sunny, dry sites

One of the key ways that plants deal with drought is by having smaller, narrower leaves. Small leaves, especially thin, needlelike ones, lose far less water than big, flat leaves with a large surface area. The leaves of Scotch broom (*Cytisus scoparius*, page 70) are virtually non-existent, for example, and are no more than tiny scales on its tough, wiry, green stems. Leaves of other drought-tolerant species may have a tough, shiny cuticle to prevent water loss, such as those of shrubby hare's ear (*Bupleurum fruticosum*, page 54).

Many plants of hot dry places have thick fleshy leaves that can actually store water—stonecrop (*Sedum spectabile*, page 124) is a typical example.

Plants with scented leaves have developed a novel method of reducing water loss. On hot days the volatile oils that give the plant its characteristic perfume evaporate from the leaves and form a protective "cloud" around the plant to keep in moisture.

A number of factors reduce the likelihood of leaves scorching in the full glare of the sun. Silver leaves reflect light so that it bounces back off the leaf without damaging it. Sometimes it's not the leaves themselves that are silver but the layer of hairs that cover them. In addition to

Brooms, such as this, Cytisus 'Burkwoodii', have adapted to life in drought conditions by evolving tough, tiny leaves that are far less vulnerable to moisture loss than larger leaves.

The silvery color of sea holly leaves (Eryngium) and the leaf-like bracts that surround the flowerheads reflect back the sun's rays and stop them damaging the leaves' internal cells.

Heathers not only have small overlapping leaves that are not harmed by strong winds, but many species also have a neat, compact, ground-hugging shape that resists damage.

29

reflecting light, hairs also shade the leaf and reduce water loss and can even combat the effects of salt damage in coastal gardens. Silver-leafed eryngium (*Eryngium bourgatii*, page 79) flourishes in dry conditions—the drier the better—and its leaves turn even more intensely silver as the environment becomes more hostile.

Plants that form a densely packed rosette of leaves—for example, hens-and-chicks (*Sempervivum tectorum*, page 127)—have also adapted to growing in full sun. The overlapping leaves shade each other and reduce water loss. You can demonstrate this by putting a pot of hens-and-chicks into a shady spot. After a while the rosettes of leaves become less densely packed.

Windy, exposed sites

Plants that have adapted to open, exposed habitats tend to have leaves that are split into small leaflets or that are feathery and finely divided. In a gale these are far less likely to be damaged than a big, flat leaf, which is easily torn.

Habitat has also shaped their overall appearance. Plants of exposed places tend to form low-growing, rounded shapes that resist the wind, with all their branches and leaves neatly tucked in, so that the wind skims right over. Out of sight, they have deep root systems that anchor them firmly in the earth.

Small species of hebe (*Hebe albicans*, page 88), with their neat, rounded shape do well on exposed coastal sites; heathers (*Erica cinerea*, page 78, and *Calluna vulgaris*, page 57) survive by similar means on exposed inland gardens.

Do not assume a plant that grows well in an exposed seaside garden will transplant equally happily to an open, windy site inland. Although coasts may be buffeted by gales, it's always a few degrees warmer on the coast because of the warming presence of the sea, which cools down more slowly in winter than the land.

Coping with shade

All plants need light to photosynthesize—that is, to produce sugars from water and carbon dioxide using the sun's energy—but their requirements vary enormously. Even some sun-loving plants will tolerate a surprising degree of shade, although they may flower less prolifically than they would in full sun, or produce less upright and more sprawling growth.

Damp shade

Shade plants that prefer damp soil often have large, thin leaves to catch maximum sunlight and rain. Those that are essentially woodland species grow quickly and flower early in the year before the tree canopy develops. Thereafter, smaller plants take a backseat—indeed, many eventually die back altogether until the following spring, including the wood anemone (*Anemone nemorosa*, page 46) and spring bulbs such as snowdrops (*Galanthus nivalis*) and woodland bluebells (*Hyacinthoides non-scripta*).

Dry shade

The combination of dry soil and shade defeats many plants in the struggle to get enough light while minimizing water loss at the same time. But there are some species that can cope. Their leaves often have a shiny surface to reflect light back onto the undersides of neighboring leaves—for example, silverberry (*Elaeagnus pungens*, page 76) or ivy (*Hedera helix*, page 89).

Water-loving plants

There are fewer telltale signs to help you identify plants that grow in permanently wet or moist soil. This is one case where you have to rely on the advice of a garden center or nursery and on reference books. Or simply look at the plants growing at the margins of a pond—whether these are native species in the wild or more formal plantings in a friend's or neighbor's garden or in the grounds of a garden that is open to the public. A plant's Latin name can often be a useful guide (see opposite).

Shade-tolerant shrubs such as Elaeagnus ebbingei 'Gilt Edge' often feature shiny, glossy leaves that reflect precious light back onto the undersides of neighboring foliage.

Anemones are typical woodland plants, flowering and making most of their growth in early spring. That way they can take advantage of maximum sunlight before trees come into full leaf.

Any plant with the word maritimus *meaning "growing by the sea" in its Latin name will do well in a coastal garden. Sea kale, otherwise known as* Crambe maritima, *is a good example.*

The clue to the forget-me-not's preferred habitat lies in the second half of its Latin name, Myosotis sylvatica. Sylvatica *means "growing in woodland and forests."*

Getting clues from Latin names

Latin names for plants can seem off-putting or intimidating. They are often long, complicated, difficult to spell, and even more difficult to pronounce. Yet apart from ensuring that you buy exactly the plant you are looking for, rather than relying on the common name, which can vary from region to region, Latin names can sometimes help you to find out more about a plant. It's the second word in the two-part name that is the more useful in this respect. The first part of the name denotes the genus the plant belongs to—a group of fairly similar plants. The second word in the Latin name is the specific name, which can give many clues to a plant's preferred habitat.

As a great part of our own language is derived from Latin, most of these words will not seem alien, and some will be familiar. You do not need a degree to translate them into some kind of working sense for gardeners.

The words listed in the box right are all adjectival, which means that the endings will vary slightly when matched to a genus, to agree with it in gender and in number. Hence sea kale is *Crambe maritima* rather than *maritimus*.

PLANT NAME CLUES	
Habitat	***Latin word* (translation)**
Wet site	*aquaticus* (living in water)
	aquatilis (living in water)
	hydrophilus (water-loving)
	pluvialis (living in rainy areas)
Dry site	*aridus* (living in dry places)
	xerophilus (dry-loving)
Sunny site	*apricus* (growing in sunny areas)
	solaris (of the sun)
Cold site	*algidus* (cold)
	frigidus (growing in cold places)
Woodland	*sylvicola* (growing in wooded areas)
	sylvatica (growing in wooded areas)
Seashore	*maritimus* (growing by the sea)
	littoralis (growing on the seashore)
	marinus (growing by the sea)
Meadow	*arvensis* (growing in cultivated fields)
Marsh	*palustris* (growing in marshes)
Sandy soil	*arenarius* (growing in sandy areas)
	arenicola (growing in sandy areas)
Chalky soil	*calcareus* (growing on chalk)
	calcicola (thriving on chalk)
Acidic soil	*calcifugus* (lime-hating)

CARING FOR PLANTS IN TOUGH SITUATIONS

Giving plants the best possible start

All the plants in the directory (pages 40—141) have been chosen for their ability to grow in tough situations, but when you are introducing small, new plants into the garden, this doesn't mean that you can simply put them in the ground and forget about them. In fact, you're not likely to get far if you do.

It's always best to start with relatively small plants that will adapt to the specific conditions in your particular garden as they grow and establish. But small plants are also the most vulnerable and do need a helping hand to get started. If you invest time and effort in giving them a good start when you plant and a bit of attention for the first year or two, then you will reap the benefits later when plants are big and well-established enough to survive without any extra attention.

Planting

Most container-grown plants can be planted out at any time that ground isn't waterlogged, frozen, or baked hard.

Bare-rooted plants (shrubs, roses, trees) are usually on sale from late autumn to early spring and should be planted as soon as possible after purchase. Look for a "tide mark" on the stem that indicates the depth the plant was growing in the soil and replant it to the same depth.

Faced with a featureless expanse of bare earth, it is tempting to ignore recommended planting distances and crowd plants together for an instant garden. But if you ignore advice, the plants will suffer as they compete for nutrients, water and space, and you'll only make more work for yourself as you'll have to separate and shift plants later on. The best way to deal with bare earth is to sow quick-growing annuals for a fast, colorful display while other species are getting established.

Get plants off to a good start by forking in a shovelful or so of well-rotted manure or garden compost at the base of the planting hole, together with a handful of slow-release fertilizer for shrubs and trees. Shovel back some of the topsoil, then set the plant on top, with its roots spead out. Finally, start to backfill the hole,

HOW TO PLANT

1. Start by digging a hole bigger than the pot the plant is growing in. Use a fork to loosen the soil at the base of the hole to help the roots penetrate. Add a generous scoop or two of well-rotted manure or compost.

2. Tap the pot gently to loosen the plant rootball and carefully tip the plant out. If it is potbound—that is, if the roots are spiraling around in a tight ball—try to gently tease roots apart, to encourage them to grow outward.

3. Lay a stick across the planting hole to make sure you replant the plant at the same depth it was growing in the pot. Then replace the soil, firming it down gently as you go, to flatten any air pockets.

sifting the soil through the roots so that no air pockets are trapped in the roots.

When planting a shrub or large plant, try to leave a shallow depression in the earth around the plant—barely 1 inch (2.5 cm) is sufficient—when you firm the soil back into the planting hole. Then, when you water the plant, the water will naturally pool around the plant before sinking down to the roots, rather than spreading further across the flowerbed and draining away from the plant.

Planting in dry, shady areas

Dry shade is one of the most difficult sites to plant in, and even though you have chosen plants that have adapted to deal with this habitat, they will still respond to a bit of cosseting and special attention in the early stages of growth. The first step is to dig in some well-rotted manure or garden compost to improve the soil. Then water the soil well before and after planting. Try mulching the soil after heavy rainfall too, to keep moisture in. If you use an organic mulch, it will also help to improve the soil when it eventually rots down.

Planting on a slope

Even though you are planting species specifically to deal with the difficulties of growing on a slope, you can still give them a helping hand. One way to help stabilize the soil is to cover it with plastic netting, secured to the ground with metal pegs or skewers. Cut a cross shape into the netting where you want to add a plant and fold back the corners to form a plant-sized hole. Once the plant is firmly in place, ease the corners of the netting back under the plant.

Use a lawn sprinkler on its gentlest setting to water a newly planted slope or you risk washing away precious topsoil. Incidentally, the soil at the base of a slope is often moist where rain water runs down and collects, so this could be the ideal spot to plant some moisture-loving species.

Planting in hot weather

In some respects planting in hot weather is a good thing, as a wilting plant is positively encouraged to take up water from the surrounding soil and may even get established faster. But a plant that is over-stressed may never fully recover, and this is when it can pay to look critically at the plant and cut off the largest leaves and flowering stems, which can make excessive demands on the root system and affect the whole plant.

If you are really worried, you can make a "shade" from a frame of sticks covered with netting until the plant gets stronger or the weather cools down.

Watering

Even drought-resistant plants need watering in their first year or two to help their roots get established. By giving these plants a helping hand while they are young, they will develop strong, healthy root systems that will subsequently deal with dry conditions all by themselves. Heathers and ferns in particular benefit from this treatment. And once they are a couple of years old they become low-maintenance plants.

A full watering can of water once a week is better than a light sprinkling every day. Watering little and often, so that the water doesn't soak down to any great depth, encourages roots to stay near the surface, instead of spreading deep and wide in search of water.

Pruning

Pruning not only shapes a plant to make it look its best, it also stimulates a plant into strong, healthy growth. Newly planted shrubs benefit from pruning. First of all snip out any dead stems. Then look for those that look spindly or weak, or where there are leaves showing signs of disease and stress. The final cuts you make should be to improve the plant's overall appearance and shape—for these cuts, prune the stems back to a fat healthy bud that faces out, away from the plant. Plants with variegated leaves may produce shoots that have reverted to the original plain green form from which they have developed. These should be pruned out immediately, as they are often stronger than the variegated form and may weaken and overtake the plant.

How to make the most of difficult conditions

In difficult conditions how you plant is important. In dry shade and where there are thirsty tree roots close to the soil surface, line the planting hole with plastic to keep water close to the plant's roots rather than the tree's. Puncture the plastic in a few places so that excess water can drain away rather than create a stagnant puddle. If the soil is shallow or if there is a real mat of tree roots, try building up informal, small, raised beds for each plant. Make a mound of topsoil and well-rotted manure or compost on the surface of the ground, and keep it in position with a ring of rocks and stones.

A gravel mulch is ideal for sunny, dry gardens and retains moisture while reflecting back the light for plants that really like it hot.

Mulching

Mulching with well-rotted manure or garden compost will help to retain moisture around

MATERIALS FOR MULCHING

Bark

Chipped bark is an organic mulch and will eventually decompose—but not for a year or two.

Black polyethylene

Polyethylene is cheap and useful for suppressing weed germination by blocking out the light. It can be hidden under a layer of bark.

Gravel

Gravel is an ideal inorganic mulch for hot, dry beds. It acts in just the same way as other mulches by preventing excess water loss.

Stones

Just a bigger version of gravel and ideal for sun-loving plants, which will appreciate the light reflected from the stones' surfaces.

Fleece

An inert layer of fleece allows moisture to penetrate but not weeds. You can always disguise it with a thin layer of bark.

Woven polypropylene

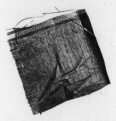

One of the toughest weed suppressants that also allows moisture through. Again, disguise it with bark if you prefer.

37

Alliums with globe-shaped flowerheads and tall, wiry-stemmed Verbena bonariensis *thrive in dry situations that would defeat lesser plants. A gravel mulch conserves what little moisture there is.*

newly planted specimens as well as suppress weeds that compete for water, nutrients, and light. In hot, dry beds an inert gravel mulch is more appropriate and sympathetic and stops water evaporating and weeds growing albeit without adding nutrients. Gravel also warms up quickly in spring, giving sun-loving plants a boost.

In winter a mulch gives plants an extra layer of insulation, and if it is deep enough can even prevent the soil from freezing, depending on how cold your winters are.

Staking

In windy seaside gardens and exposed inland areas, young trees and shrubs are going to need staking for a few years until their roots are strong enough to anchor them to the soil.

When you are choosing a stake do not settle for one that is much taller than the plant. The aim of using a stake is to give a shrub or tree some support until the roots can take over the job. A small stake that holds the lower portion of the stem or trunk steady while letting the branches move freely in the wind will encourage the stem to thicken and the roots to spread out to hold the plant in the soil.

Hammer the stake into the planting hole before you plant so you do not damage the roots. Use a proper tree tie to hold the stem in place. If you prefer to improvise, use something soft, like cut-up strips of rag. Do not use wire and string, which can cut into bark and stems. Check ties twice a year in autumn and spring and loosen if necessary as the trunk grows thicker.

Perennials can often do with a bit of support on windy sites too, or even just to stop them bending after heavy rain. Whichever method you choose (see below), get the support system into the ground at the same time as you plant the

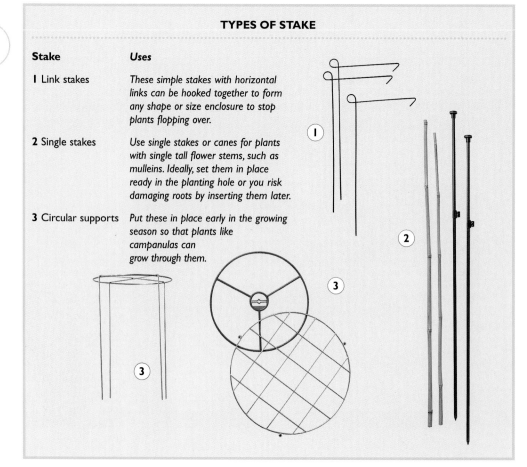

TYPES OF STAKE

Stake	Uses
1 Link stakes	*These simple stakes with horizontal links can be hooked together to form any shape or size enclosure to stop plants flopping over.*
2 Single stakes	*Use single stakes or canes for plants with single tall flower stems, such as mulleins. Ideally, set them in place ready in the planting hole or you risk damaging roots by inserting them later.*
3 Circular supports	*Put these in place early in the growing season so that plants like campanulas can grow through them.*

plant—that way you avoid damaging its root system. The one exception is if you choose twiggy prunings from other plants tucked in among perennials to keep them upright, as these rarely need to be pushed too far into the ground and can be angled away from the plant's roots.

Controlling tough plants

In some circumstances a tough plant can become so successful that it is almost a nuisance, particularly if it is smothering smaller plants in an effort to get established. Plants that self-seed prolifically are relatively easy to deal with. Cutting off the spent flowerheads will prevent them setting seed. Plants that spread by runners underground can be stopped by a vertical layer of slates, tiles, or bricks embedded in the border.

Some plants are banned altogether in certain American states and Canadian provinces, where they are known as "noxious plants", as they can grow out of control and become dangerous. Noxious plants and the areas in which they are banned are detailed in the plant directory. Some areas will impose penalties, so contact your state or regional agriculture or plant extension office for additional information.

Frost protection

New plants that haven't made sufficient root growth can often be lifted out of the ground by a severe frost. When the soil freezes it expands, sometimes with enough force to lift a small plant along with it. After severe weather, walk around the garden, and gently firm any affected plants back into place. If severe weather is forecast, prepare in advance and cover vulnerable new plants with newspaper weighed down with bricks, old sheets, or horticultural fleece.

39

Left: Plants that are set out late in the season may suffer frost damage. This is also true of some plants before they mature. If you are in any doubt, protect the vulnerable crown of a plant at soil level with a thick layer of straw or horticultural fleece. Folding or tying last year's leaves in place over the crown will also give protection to plants like this yucca.

How to use the directory

The plants in the directory are listed alphabetically by Latin name. When you are looking at the entry for a plant, be sure to fold out the extended back flap of the book cover. This will give you an instant guide to the planting symbols (see below) shown immediately below the plant's common name. You'll have all the information you need at your fingertips, to tell you whether this is a plant for a sloping border, sun or shade, dry soil or waterlogged, and so on.

Each entry includes a short description of each plant and describes how it has adapted to suit the particular conditions it grows in. In some cases information on closely related alternative species is also given. Brief details on planting and plant care are also included.

SITUATION

These symbols give a general indication of the problem situations that a plant will grow well in.

 Exposed garden

 Sloping garden

 Bog garden

 Coastal garden

MICROCLIMATE

These symbols indicate the extreme conditions a plant has evolved to cope with—some are able to cope with a range of these tough conditions.

 Moist, damp conditions

 Dry, drought conditions

 Sunny conditions

 Shady conditions

SOIL pH

If your soil has a high or low pH, choose plants that will flourish in particularly acidic or alkaline soil.

 Acidic soil

 Alkaline soil

TYPE OF SOIL

Once you have ascertained what type of soil you have, use these symbols to choose the plants that will thrive in your garden.

Stony soil

Clay soil

Sandy soil

Chalky soil

Poor soil

Any soil

ZONE CHART

ZONE 5–8 Zones designate the lowest range of temperatures in which a plant will normally survive. Thus a plant in Zone 8 will normally survive between 10°F and 20°F (-12°C and -6°C).

ZONE	°FAHRENHEIT	°CENTIGRADE
1	Below -50	Below -45
2	-50 to -40	-45 to -40
3	-40 to -30	-40 to -34
4	-30 to -20	-34 to -29
5	-20 to -10	-29 to -23
6	-10 to 0	-23 to -18
7	0 to 10	-18 to -12
8	10 to 20	-12 to -6
9	20 to 30	-6 to -1
10	30 to 40	-1 to 5
11	above 40	above 5

Achillea filipendulina

Yarrow

ZONE
3–10

Achillea filipendulina is a type of yarrow, a tough wildflower of open fields and wastelands. It has finely cut, fernlike, soft green leaves. In summer it produces great flat heads of intense gold flowers on erect stalks, to 5 feet (1.5 m) tall, and carries on flowering well into autumn.

Look out, too, for other cultivars, such as *A. filipendulina* 'Cloth of Gold' (slightly smaller with big flowerheads) and 'Gold Plate' (just a little smaller and with grayer leaves).

WHERE TO PLANT

These plants will flourish in hot, dry sites and on sandy or thin chalky soils. The tough, wiry stems rarely need staking, even in exposed, windy sites or seaside gardens, yet they are flexible enough to bend and twist in the wind without snapping. Plant with other tough, summer-flowering perennials, such as poppies (*Papaver orientale*) and helenium hybrids, for a classic herbaceous border, plus some showy stonecrop (*Sedum spectabile*) for late summer color.

CARING FOR PLANTS

To give them the best start, set out young plants in early spring. When older clumps start to get congested, flowering more densely around the edge than the center (which usually happens after three or four years), they should be divided. Lift the clump, split it, and replant the pieces separately, discarding any woody bits from the center. Ideally, do this straight after flowering or in early spring, just as the plant is coming into growth.

43

The large, flat flowerheads of Achillea filipendulina *attract bees, butterflies, and other beneficial insects into the garden, as well as being good cut flowers, fresh or dried.*

Alchemilla mollis

Lady's mantle

Its low-growing, clump-forming habit and the soft downy hairs on its leaves make lady's mantle a tough and adaptable plant. It's also pretty, with modest sprays of tiny, greenish-yellow flowers all summer long.

WHERE TO PLANT
Lady's mantle can cope with an enormous range of situations. It is not fussy about soil—growing in sand, chalk, or clay—as long as it is not waterlogged. It thrives in both shade and hot sun, brightening the shade under trees and pushing up through unforgiving, sun-baked gravel. The low, rounded clumps resist the damaging effects of wind in exposed sites and seaside gardens.

CARING FOR PLANTS
Lady's mantle needs little attention, apart from dividing clumps when they get too big. Watch for self-sown seedlings and move them to more suitable positions if necessary. To avoid self-seeding, cut off the flowerheads before the seed has a chance to ripen.

Lady's mantle (Alchemilla mollis) *has a froth of subtle greeny yellow flowers that set off more gaudy blooms to perfection.*

Allium atropurpureum

Allium, ornamental onion

These bulbs belong to the same genus as onions, and you will notice this at once if you bruise a leaf and smell that familiar aroma. Most species like hot, dry conditions. *Allium atropurpureum* is one of the easiest to grow; it has heads of starry, purplish-red flowers in early summer, borne on erect stems to 3 feet (1 m) tall. Like most other alliums, it has long, strap-shaped leaves, which have a tendency to wither away before the flowers appear. Also look out for *A. cernuum*, which has loose, nodding heads of pink flowers, and *A. flavum*, which is lower growing and has yellow flowers. Pale lavender *A. hollandicum* will colonize a sunny bank.

WHERE TO PLANT
A. atropurpureum will cope with dry, sun-baked earth and free-draining, sandy soils. Because the leaves tend to look untidy, mix it in with foliage plants that will disguise this habit. As long as the leaves have a reasonable amount of sun early in the growing season, it will not matter if they are shaded by neighboring plants later on.

CARING FOR PLANTS
Plant bulbs of *A. atropurpureum* in autumn. Plant any allium bulbs twice as deep as the width of the bulb.

Planting in autumn into an established border or bed helps you visualize more easily the impact the alliums will have when they are in full flower. Well-established clumps of allium bulbs can be divided in autumn, after flowering.

The flowerheads of Allium atropurpureum *are shuttlecock-shaped rather than the more typically spherical heads of other allium species.*

44

Anemone nemorosa

Wood anemone

ZONE
5–9

As its name suggests, the wood anemone is a woodland plant. It thrives in early-season sun, before the tree canopy bursts into leaf, and thereafter enjoys the dappled shade of the leaf cover. It is low growing, with delicate, whitish, drooping flowers in spring. Wood anemones have deeply divided leaves and spread quickly to produce a carpet of groundcover.

Cultivars developed from the species include *A. nemorosa* 'Robinsonia', which has lavender flowers, and 'Blue Beauty', which has blue flowers and bronze-tinged foliage.

WHERE TO PLANT

Look for shady spots in the garden that mimic deciduous woodland—beneath shrubs or trees, for example, or in areas shaded by fences, sheds, and other manmade structures. Take advantage of the anemone's quick-spreading nature to create a weedfree, groundcover carpet.

CARING FOR PLANTS

Plant rhizomes in autumn. If possible, dig in some well-rotted manure or some leaf mold to give them a good start. Add a mulch of leaf mold again in spring, especially if your anemones are growing in borders shaded by buildings, rather than under trees or shrubs, to mimic more closely woodland conditions. Autumn is also the best time to divide large clumps.

Anemone nemorosa 'Royal Blue' is a cultivated variety of the wild wood anemone and has blue flowers rather than the white of the species.

46

Anthemis punctata subsp. cupianana

Anthemis

ZONE
4–9

Anthemis punctata subsp. *cupianana* is a fairly small plant, which forms a dense evergreen mat. It has pleasantly aromatic, silver-gray foliage. In summer it blooms with a great flush of daisylike, white flowers with yellow centers that last and last. In a temperate winter the foliage dulls to a gray-green but does not die away.

WHERE TO PLANT

Because it never grows higher than about 1 foot (30 cm), anthemis is best planted at the edge of a border or along a path. Set out young plants in spring in a hot, sunny position. The plants do not mind chalky or sandy soil. Their mat-forming habit and silver summer foliage make them ideal in seaside gardens, although they do prefer a spot in the shelter of larger plants if possible. They also do well in containers.

CARING FOR PLANTS

To keep anthemis plants growing vigorously, cut them back hard after flowering or, at the very least, snip off the flowering stems. Failure to do so can actually shorten the life of the plant.

If you are worried about a plant's vigor, take cuttings of young shoots in spring and grow them on in pots for replacements.

Plants can be divided into smaller clumps if they grow too large; this can be done in spring or in autumn.

47

The appealing daisylike flowers of anthemis look good massed in pots and planters. It is a plant for hot, sunny sites and does well in seaside gardens.

Astilbe chinensis var. pumila

Astilbe

ZONE
6–10

Astilbes have fernlike leaves and plumes of tiny flowers held on erect, wiry stems. *A. chinensis* var. *pumila* has flowers in a surprising shade of mauve, and some cultivars have flower spikes that look as if they have been dipped in red dye.

WHERE TO PLANT
Astilbes need moisture all year, so be sure of your site before planting. If your damp patch is just a seasonal problem that dries up in summer, so will the astilbe, and it will probably give up growing altogether if it remains dry for too long. If the soil is truly waterlogged, the plants will even be able to tolerate some sun.

Set out young plants in autumn or spring and give them a mulch of well-rotted manure or garden compost to keep the soil extra moist while the plants are getting established.

CARING FOR PLANTS
Occasionally, late frosts can scorch off all the flower buds. If an unseasonable frost is predicted, try to protect new buds and leaves with a layer of straw, newspaper, or plastic. When a clump develops a bald center, lift and divide it, discarding the central portion.

The startling mauve plumes of Astilbe chinensis var. pumila *never need staking and form interesting seedheads when the flowers have finished.*

Aubrieta deltoidea

Aubrieta

pH

ZONE
4–9

In some areas, cascades of intense purple or cerise flowers on old garden walls are a sure sign of spring. Aubrieta plants form great, ground-hugging mats of color. All hybrids come from the original species, *A. deltoidea*, which is itself quite variable. The flower colors range from white to violet, and some are tinged with red. They are simple, four-petaled flowers, but massed together in a mature plant they create a huge impact of color.

WHERE TO PLANT
Aubrietas come from dry, rocky, mountain slopes in the Middle East and are perfectly at home rooting in tiny cracks in paving or gaps where mortar has fallen from a low wall. They tend to be too vigorous for a rockery full of alpines and are better used to soften hard-edged landscaping. Do not plant them directly on a paved path as they will simply get trod upon—they are not as tough as thyme, for example, and cannot survive heavy foot traffic.

CARING FOR PLANTS
Clipping mats of aubrieta with garden shears after flowering promotes healthy growth and stops plants from becoming too straggly, with bare bases and all the growth clustered at the extreme ends of the stems. Aubrieta will often self-seed, and the seedlings should be transplanted when they are small and before they have time to wedge themselves firmly into inaccessible crevices.

The cultivar Aubrieta 'Dr. Mules' *has single flowers in an intense shade of violet that smother the plant with color for weeks in spring.*

49

Aucuba japonica

Japanese laurel

50

ZONE
7–10

It is probably its adaptability that causes some people to sneer at the Japanese laurel. It can grow just about anywhere, particularly in neglected corners, and it may well appear miserable simply through its association with such less pleasant spots. It is, in fact, a very useful shrub that will grow to a rounded bush about 10 feet (3 m) tall. It can also be planted to create a dense and private hedge.

WHERE TO PLANT

If you must have a plant at all costs in a gray, sunless corner of the garden with soil so poor that even the weeds struggle to grow, Japanese laurel is for you. It will put up with just about anything, apart from permanently waterlogged soil, and its glossy evergreen leaves will reflect the light and look handsome all year. If you choose a cultivar of *A. japonica* with variegated leaves, such as 'Crotonifolia' or 'Gold Dust', you will need to make sure it gets a reasonable amount of sun each day to keep its variegation or the leaves will eventually revert to plain green.

CARING FOR PLANTS

To get the characteristic, cheerful red berries in autumn you need a female plant with a male one in close proximity, your own or one in a neighboring garden. If you spot any plain green leaves on variegated cultivars, cut the stems right back to the base to stop the plant from reverting.

The Japanese laurel is dioecious, which means that male and female flowers grow on separate plants. Only the female plant bears the attractive, long-lasting autumn berries, but there must first be a male plant in the vicinity to pollinate it.

Berberis thunbergii

Japanese berberry

ZONE
4–10

There are both evergreen and deciduous species of Japanese berberry, but the deciduous ones, such as *B. thunbergii*, have intensely colored foliage in autumn. The leaves of the form *atropurpurea*, for example, are normally purplish-red, but they turn a vivid red before they drop. At the same time you should get a colorful crop of small, shiny, red berries.

WHERE TO PLANT

This Japanese berberry is a dense, thorny shrub, which makes an ideal shelter for more delicate plants. It also makes a tough property hedge, especially as it eventually grows to 5 feet (1.5 m) or more. When planting as a hedge or windbreak, set out young plants 18 inches (45 cm) apart and put up a temporary screen, such as some netting or trellis, to protect them until the roots get well established. Cut off between a third and a quarter of the top growth to encourage them to bush out.

CARING FOR PLANTS

Japanese berberry can be grown as an informal or a formal hedge, left to spread out or clipped into a neat shape. To keep an informal hedge full of healthy, strong shoots, take out any very old or straggly stems at the end of winter before the shrubs come into flower or later on, in summer, after flowering.

Severe weather enhances the autumn color of the leaves of Berberis thunbergii f. atropurpurea, *which turn bright red before they eventually drop.*

51

Brachyglottis monroi (syn. Senecio monroi)

Brachyglottis

ZONE 7–10

Brachyglottis monroi puts up with fierce sunshine and regular wind. It is a small, rounded shrub, to about 3 feet (1 m) tall and across, with gray-green leaves that are thickly felted with white underneath.

WHERE TO PLANT

Plant a row of brachyglottis in spring to provide shelter for more vulnerable plants. Set them out about 18 inches (45 cm) apart and protect the plants with a temporary windbreak in the first year or two until the roots have had time to take a firm hold. Thereafter they will do the job of windbreak for you. Make sure you choose a spot in full sun. If you want to use brachyglottis as a privacy hedge, look out for B. Dunedin Hybrid 'Sunshine' (syn. *Senecio* 'Sunshine'), which grows to 5 feet (1.5 m) tall.

CARING FOR PLANTS

Trim back bushes lightly after flowering to tidy them up or prune them more severely for a formal appearance. For an extra flush of new growth, cut back plants hard in spring.

Brachyglottis are a native New Zealand species, making them sun loving, fairly hardy, and able to survive in windy, exposed sites.

Buddleja davidii

Butterfly bush

pH   ZONE 5–10

This species of *Buddleja* has long, arching stems and leaves that are long, pointed, and downy, with white undersides. In summer it is smothered in graceful drooping spires of flowerheads packed with tiny flowers rich in nectar. One of the bonuses of the plant is that in addition to putting up with some awkward sites and conditions, it attracts masses of insects, particularly butterflies, to the garden. Lots of cultivars have been developed from the original species, which has pale purple flowers. *B. davidii* 'Empire Blue' has purple-blue flowers, 'Black Knight' has deep purple flowers, and 'Royal Red' has reddish-purple flowers. Cultivars are usually smaller than the species, which can reach 10-15 feet (3-4.5 m).

WHERE TO PLANT

Buddleia bushes can be quick to colonize vacant lots. Take advantage of their tolerant, fast-growing nature and use them to create sheltered corners in an exposed garden or to make a patch of summer shade in an open space.

CARING FOR PLANTS

Butterfly bushes grow so fast that they can soon look messy if you do not keep an eye on them. Cut them back hard in spring, taking back every soft green shoot to within a few inches (several centimeters) of the hard, woody stems. This will ensure the best possible display of flowers and foliage. An unseasonable frost may scorch young leaves and buds, but plants soon recover.

The flower spikes of the butterfly bush can be up to 15 inches (38 cm) long. Each individual floret is tubular in shape and holds a drop of nectar.

Bupleurum fruticosum

Shrubby hare's ear

ZONE 7–10

Shrubby hare's ear has glossy, blue-green, evergreen leaves and is studded with masses of tiny, star-shaped, yellow-green flowers all through the summer and into autumn.

WHERE TO PLANT
The tough, leathery leaves of *Bupleurum* resist the drying effects of wind and sun and will even withstand salt-laden winds. These same properties also help it resist polluted city atmospheres, where grit-laden winds can damage less well-armored leaves. Because it is initially low-growing and spreads quickly, *Bupleurum* is useful as a shrubby groundcover, its dense habit effectively choking weeds. It will grow to 5 feet (1.5 m) if left unpruned.

CARING FOR PLANTS
Cut away any untidy shoots in mid- to late spring and any stems that have suffered scorching or the effects of a severe winter. To get a flush of completely fresh new growth and to keep plants small, shrubby hare's ear can also be pruned hard at this time of year.

Shrubby hare's ear has a long flowering season. Its blooms are curiosities rather than showstoppers, but are popular as cut flowers.

Calendula officinalis

Calendula, pot marigold

ZONE 6–10

The cheerful marigold needs no introduction. So commonplace, it is easy to take it for granted, but it is a useful, undemanding plant for a quick burst of color. Many cultivars have been developed from the original species, and you can now get flowers in shades of apricot, yellow, and cream, as well as the original orange. The species has single, daisylike flowers, but many of the cultivars have double flowers packed with petals. They flower all summer long. The species is fairly compact, growing to 12—18 inches (30—45 cm) tall, but some of the cultivars are taller.

WHERE TO PLANT
Marigolds will flower best in full sun, but they still put on a reasonable display in light shade. Like many other hardy annuals valued for their flowers, poor, stony soil presents no problem to marigolds, and rich, fertile soil actually reduces the number of flowers they produce. Plant marigolds in soil that has been spoiled by construction rubble or where you need a temporary filler in a bed until you can improve the soil.

CARING FOR PLANTS
If you are sowing marigold seeds directly into the soil—it can germinate within a week—then watch out for slugs and snails while the seedlings are still small. Once they are larger the odd nibbled leaf is less noticeable and less devastating. Rub off any greenfly infestations as soon as you spot them.

Successive sowings of marigold seed at intervals from spring until early summer will ensure a display of flowers until well into autumn.

Calluna vulgaris 'Yellow One'

Scotch heather

Although heathers are generally appreciated as a swathe of color, if you get up close to a plant you will see that the flower spikes are pretty. The fringes of the individual flower bells may be tipped with color or the stamens may hang below the petals and provide an attractive contrast.

Calluna vulgaris is the common wild heather, and hundreds of cultivars have been developed from it, ranging from low-growing, creeping plants to taller specimens up to 2 feet (60 cm) tall. 'Yellow One' has pink flowers in early to mid-autumn and yellow foliage in summer, which turns red in autumn; it grows to about 12 inches (30 cm) tall and 18 inches (45 cm) across. 'Sunset Glow' has white flowers in late summer to early autumn and lime green foliage in summer, which turns yellow in autumn; it grows to about 8 inches (20 cm) tall and 2 feet (60 cm) across.

WHERE TO PLANT
Plant heathers in an open, sunny spot well away from deciduous trees: nothing spoils a display quite as much as fallen leaves caught among the stems. *Calluna* is native to acidic moorlands and is ideal for gardens with acidic soil; it will not do well in areas where the soil is alkaline.

CARING FOR PLANTS
Keep an eye on new plants and do not let them dry out. Water them thoroughly in dry spells until the plants are a couple of years old, by which time they will have developed extensive roots that will cope with any subsequent dry weather. Lightly clip plants in early spring, just before they come into growth. Be prepared to replace old plants after six or seven years; it is a good idea to have some summer cuttings waiting in reserve.

The new summer foliage of Calluna vulgaris *'Yellow One' is a cheerful shade of yellow and then changes color in autumn as the temperature drops.*

Caltha palustris

Marsh marigold

When in flower, it's easy to see that the marsh marigold is part of the buttercup family. The bright yellow, cup-shaped flowers are produced in spring alongside dark green, glossy leaves. Plants form large clumps after a few years, up to 16 inches (40 cm) tall and 18 inches (45 cm) across. Some naturally occurring varieties have white flowers, and cultivated forms include 'Flore Pleno', which has double yellow flowers.

WHERE TO PLANT
Marsh marigolds are native to boggy areas and are ideal for wet ditches and troughs. They can also be grown in the damp margins of a pond or in water, as long as it is no deeper than about 6 inches (15 cm). What you cannot do is grow them in variable soil that is wet after heavy rain but dries out in periods of dry weather; plants must be permanently damp even if not actually waterlogged.

CARING FOR PLANTS
When clumps outgrow their situation, divide them up into smaller portions. Do this either when they have finished flowering or in autumn as growth is slowing down.

57

The flowers of the marsh marigold cultivar 'Flore Pleno' have been selected for their double habit. They are followed by pod-shaped seed capsules.

Camellia x williamsii

Camellia

Camellia x williamsii is one of the most easily grown camellias and one of the most reliable bloomers. Most of the cultivars have narrow, oval leaves and make tall, densely packed shrubs. The flowers vary in color from white to deep red and may be single or semi-double.

'Crinkles' has large semi-double flowers in a delicate shade of rose-pink. Another cultivar worth growing is 'Anticipation', which has deep pink blooms reminiscent of peony flowers, with a central boss of stamens. It is particularly recommended for containers and pots, making it suitable for small gardens, although if grown directly in the soil it can get up to 10 feet (3 m).

The weather determines precisely when in spring they flower, and a late winter can delay blooming by up to a month.

WHERE TO PLANT
Many people go to great lengths to grow camellias in tubs and raised beds to create the acidic soil they prefer, so if you have got acidic soil, you're one step ahead and the envy of many gardening friends. The one proviso is to choose a spot in the garden that doesn't get the early morning sun. Although plants are reliably hardy, after a spring frost frozen flower buds can be damaged by thawing too quickly in strong sunlight.

CARING FOR PLANTS
Deadheading after flowering promotes strong growth, but no pruning is necessary other than to cut out spindly shoots or to reshape the odd branch. Mulching once or twice a year after a good downpour helps prevent the roots from drying out.

Camellia x williamsii 'Crinkles' takes its name from the unusual crinkled texture of its petals. The large flowers are semi-double.

Campanula persicifolia

Peach-leafed bellflower

This perennial has the classic, bell-shaped, purple flowers that typify the genus. The flowers, at up to 2 inches (5 cm) long, are relatively large for a campanula. It has slim, upright stems, studded with flowers throughout summer. There are many cultivars, including 'Boule de Neige', with double white flowers, and 'Pride of Exmouth', with pale blue flowers.

WHERE TO PLANT
Tough enough to put up with clay soils that crack in summer, this campanula is also tolerant of varying light, from full sun to medium shade. Its basal rosette of leaves can also help to stabilize a bare slope, paving the way for other plants once the soil has settled.

59

CARING FOR PLANTS
The flowering stems may need staking in open situations. If you cut them back after flowering you often get more flowers, but if you leave them to set seed you will get plenty more seedlings for next year. Plants also have a curious habit of producing one or two more new flowers alongside the ripening seed pods, making it even more difficult to decide whether to deadhead or not.

The peach-leafed bellflower can put up with a variety of garden conditions, from full sun to shade, and will usually self-seed if a site is to its liking.

Centranthus ruber

Red valerian

ZONE
5–10

The leaves of red valerian have a grayish tinge that hints at their tolerance of hot, sunny places, as does their thickened, rather fleshy appearance. In late spring and summer and on into autumn plants bear clusters of tiny, red, nectar-rich flowers, which attract butterflies and moths. There is also a white-flowered cultivar, 'Albus', and cultivars with flowers in various shades of red-pink.

WHERE TO PLANT

Red valerian is a common sight on limestone cliffs by the sea and translates easily into similar garden situations. It puts up with chalky and sandy soils and can find a foothold in crevices in old walls or paving. If you offer it a better position in a border it generally does less well, producing floppy growth and fewer flowers.

CARING FOR PLANTS

Cutting the flowers—either after they have finished or for arranging in water—encourages more flowers to form. At the end of the season, leave some to set seed for a stock of future plants.

This is the white-flowered cultivar of valerian, Centranthus ruber *'Albus'. The difficult conditions of an old stone wall mimic its natural cliff habitat.*

Cerastium tomentosum

Snow-in-summer

ZONE
2–8

Snow-in-summer is a vigorous mat-forming perennial. It has narrow leaves and stems, and both are so densely furred with hairs that they look white from a distance. In late spring and summer it has masses of white, starry flowers, rarely more than 8 inches (20 cm) tall.

WHERE TO PLANT

Its rampant spreading habit makes it ideal for stabilizing and disguising a bank of dry soil or for covering up a less-than-beautiful wall. On level ground its dense growth makes it an effective weed-suppressing mat, especially as the leaves are evergreen, but keep it away from less vigorous species, which may get swamped.

CARING FOR PLANTS

Plants need little attention, but clipping lightly after flowering will keep them in good shape. Keep them in check by digging up and dividing as necessary, either in spring or late in summer.

61

Snow-in-summer is a typical mat-forming species that roots as it spreads, making it an ideal groundcover plant on poor dry soils.

Chaenomeles × superba

Japonica, flowering quince

ZONE 4–9

This hybrid is a rather overlooked shrub, typical of suburban gardens. Yet it has a distinctly oriental pedigree, its parents being native to China and Japan. In spring it has cup-shaped blossoms, which come in various colors, ranging from orange and shading through red to pink and occasionally white. Named cultivars are more reliably consistent in color. The other common species, C. japonica and C. speciosa are equally useful in the garden. All japonicas are capable of producing applelike fruits, which do not seem to be of interest to birds or other wildlife, although they look attractive on the shrub, especially as they ripen with a golden flush.

WHERE TO PLANT
Japonicas' lack of fussiness about soil types and light levels makes them very useful. Although you might get more flowers on plants in a sunnier spot, they still flower reliably in the shade. Shrubs can be trained on wires against a cheerless north-facing wall or incorporated into hedges.

CARING FOR PLANTS
Prune wall-trained shrubs in spring by cutting back side branches to two or three buds. Otherwise, confine pruning to thinning out tangled branches or to keeping a shrub within bounds.

Though flower color can vary, the flowers of Chaenomeles × superba *all have prominent, contrasting yellow stamens.*

Choisya ternata

Mexican orange blossom

ZONE 7–11

Choisya ternata grows rapidly to form a bushy shrub as wide as it is high, and established plants can get to 10ft (3m) tall. The glossy, evergreen leaves have a pleasant scent when crushed, and in spring the clusters of small white flowers have a delicious citrus perfume.

WHERE TO PLANT
It is unfussy about soil type, being able to cope with thin, chalky soils or clay that bakes hard in summer. 'Sundance', the golden-leafed cultivar of *C. ternata*, really does need full sun to keep its vibrant gold color, but the ordinary species can be grown in a shady corner. Plant choisya as a shrub or use it as part of a mixed hedge.

CARING FOR PLANTS
Plant new shrubs in spring so that they have all summer and autumn to get established and firmly rooted before winter. On exposed sites, frosts can scorch new growth, but plants generally recover. There is no need to prune unless the plant oversteps its boundaries.

Choisya ternata 'Sundance' needs full sun to keep its golden color, but even so it eventually fades as the foliage grows older.

Cistus x cyprius

Rock rose, sun rose

ZONE
7–9

This hybrid rock rose has large, papery, white flowers in summer. Each petal is splashed with a blotch of deep purplish-red at the base, which highlights a boss of yellow stamens. The leaves have a strong balsamic fragrance, which is released on hot days or if you rub a leaf between your fingers. It spreads rapidly to form a nicely rounded shrub, which can ultimately be about 6ft (1.5m) tall and across. Rock roses are not reliably hardy, and they are often fairly short-lived.

WHERE TO PLANT
Rock roses grow wild all over Mediterranean countries and are adapted to harsh, sunny climates. Plant *C. x cyprius* on open, sunny ground, in poor or sandy soil, and it will flourish. Its height when fully grown helps to protect smaller plants by acting as a windbreak in exposed gardens. Get new plants into the ground in spring so they are well established by winter.

CARING FOR PLANTS
Deadheading will keep a rock rose flowering for longer as well as improve its appearance. It shouldn't need pruning, but any dead or spindly branches can be cut out in spring.

Take cuttings in summer as a safeguard against plant loss in severe winter weather.

Rock roses are evergreen, retaining their leaves all year round. In full sun Cistus x cyprius *will be smothered with bold white flowers in summer.*

64

Clematis montana

Clematis

ZONE
4–9

Clematis montana is one of the toughest clematis. It flowers furiously and briefly in late spring and early summer, producing a great froth of white flowers. Other cultivars have been bred from the species. 'Elizabeth' has pink flowers and is vanilla-scented, and 'Mayleen' and 'Odorata' are also pink and fragrant. Clematis can look a bit unsightly, like a giant, untidy bird's nest in winter, but many gardeners are prepared to put up with this for its moment of flowering glory.

WHERE TO PLANT

Bleak, bare walls, unsightly garages and ugly sheds would all benefit from a curtain of *C. montana*. All clematis prefer their roots to be kept cool, with their heads in the sun. If it is growing against a wall, set the plant at least 18in (45cm) away so that it gets maximum rainfall; this is especially important if it is grown against the wall of a house with overhanging eaves. Plant in spring for the best chance of establishment before winter. *C. montana* can grow enormous with time, so choose the spot with care. It can spread to 15ft (4.5m) and climb more than twice as high.

CARING FOR PLANTS

Spring-flowering clematis like *C. montana* need little pruning, but if it does start to outgrow its situation lightly trim it back immediately after flowering. Give plants a mulch of well-rotted manure or garden compost in spring.

Cultivars of Clematis montana *have been bred with pink flowers and fragrance. Although all montanas flower only briefly, many gardeners think the display is still worth it.*

Cosmos bipinnatus

Cosmos

ZONE
8–11

Cosmos have bright green, feathery leaves and saucer-shaped flowers, which can be up to 4in (10cm) across, in colors ranging from deep pink to white. The only way you can be certain of color is by choosing a named cultivar. 'Sonata White', has white flowers, and other cultivars come in a similar range of colors to the species: 'Sea Shells' can be pink or white, and the flowers have fluted petals; 'Sensation' has bigger flowers in red, pink, or white.

WHERE TO PLANT
Despite their delicate appearance, cosmos grow well on exposed sites because their flexible, feathery leaves are far less prone to tearing in strong winds than larger, flatter leaves would be. Poor soil and dry conditions will not affect their performance. In fact, if the soil is too good you will get fewer flowers and excess foliage.

CARING FOR PLANTS
Sow seeds when there's no danger of frost and thin the seedlings out to about 12in (30cm) apart. Regular deadheading keeps plants in flower until the first frost cuts them down, but if you want some self-seeded plants for next year, leave a few seedheads to ripen and shed seed.

If your border is color themed, buy seeds of named varieties of cosmos or you could end up with a random mixture of reds, pinks, and whites. Cosmos 'Sonata Pink', pictured, is reliably pink.

Cotoneaster horizontalis

Rock cotoneaster, rockspray

ZONE
5–10

This cotoneaster is an unassuming little shrub, tenacious in its ability to grow in inhospitable sites. The genus also contains some evergreen species. *C. dammeri* grows in similar habitats to *C. horizontalis* and is similarly useful but low-growing, to 3–4in (8–10cm) maximum.

WHERE TO PLANT
As its name suggests, *C. horizontalis* spreads wider than it grows upward. It will likely not grow more than 3ft (1m) high but may spread to 5ft (1.5m). It can grow well in dry shade, on bare slopes, and against cold north walls. It often self-seeds in unlikely places, saving you the job of deciding where to put it.

CARING FOR PLANTS
There shouldn't be any need to prune shrubs, but if you need to take out any awkward branches do this in late winter. Get new plants into the ground in spring to help them become established before winter.

The twiggy framework of the rock cotoneaster has been likened to a herringbone pattern, which is even more obvious after leaf drop.

67

Crambe maritima

Sea kale

ZONE
5–9

Sea kale has large, blue-green leaves, which are crinkled and twisted just like vegetable kale. In fact, if you can spare a few plants, they make good eating, especially if blanched and cooked when young and tender. To get the full effect of the flowers, however, you will have to leave them alone. In early summer they are a mass of tiny white flowers, sweetly honey-scented, on stems around 3ft (1m) tall.

C. cordifolia is a cultivated garden species. It is much taller—to 8 ft (2.4m)—but still suitable for sunny seaside gardens. In bloom, its huge, airy flowerheads make a haze of petals and fine, thin stems.

WHERE TO PLANT
In the wild, sea kale sends up shoots on beaches above the tide line. In the garden put it in a gravel bed, on poor, stony soil, or in free-draining, sandy soil. The leaves die back after flowering quite early on in the summer, so make sure there are some neighboring plants that can spread out and cover up any subsequent gaps.

CARING FOR PLANTS
Give sea kale plants plenty of space, setting them at least 3ft (1m) apart in spring. Keep an eye out for slugs when seedlings are still tender and vulnerable. Older plants can also be divided at this time of year.

Sea kale flowers early in the summer. Sow seed under glass in spring, then plant out the seedlings when they are strong enough to survive outside.

68

Crataegus monogyna

Hawthorn

ZONE
4–9

Hawthorn is most often grown as a hedge, although left unpruned it will develop into a small tree. It has small, lobed leaves and in spring is covered with small, white flowers with an almost overpowering sickly sweet smell. These are followed by red berries (haws) in autumn. For a red-flowered version, look out for *C. laevigata* 'Paul's Scarlet', which has double flowers; 'Rosea Flore Pleno' has double pink flowers. Both are just as tough as the common singleseed.

WHERE TO PLANT
Hawthorn is densely branched and spiny, making it ideal for a boundary hedge on an exposed site. Use it to create a shelter in a seaside garden for more vulnerable species, or grow a single specimen as a tree in an open, sunny site, where it will make a traditional standard and may top 30ft (10m) after 20 years or so.

In a wildlife garden, hawthorn trees or bushes will provide protected nesting sites for birds in spring and a good food supply of berries later in the year.

CARING FOR PLANTS
If you want to try raising plants from seed, sow ripe berries in pots and leave them outside all winter. Plants get the best start if they are planted in winter as bare-root saplings. To make an impenetrable hedge, set them 1ft (30cm) apart and place a second, staggered row in front. To keep a hedge in check, clip it after flowering if possible, although winter trimming will do.

Hawthorn is prone to fireblight. Every year, prune out and burn all dead, or damaged branches, cutting at least 10–12in (25–30cm) below the damaged area. Avoid excessive nitrogen fertilizing.

The dense white blossoms of hawthorn are a sure sign of spring. In some areas it is considered unlucky to cut and bring them indoors.

69

Cyclamen hederifolium

Baby cyclamen

ZONE 3–9

The flowers of this hardy cyclamen appear before the leaves and cover the ground with pale or deep pink, occasionally white, flowers in late summer and autumn. The flowers have elegantly reflexed petals, and when the seed pods ripen the flower stalks corkscrew toward the ground before bursting to scatter the seeds. The flowers are followed by deep green, heart-shaped leaves that can last throughout the winter to fade at the end of spring.

WHERE TO PLANT

Cyclamen do well in dry shade. Plant tubers in fall under shrubs or trees for a carpet of silvery green leaves. The canopy of overhead leaves will protect the tubers from excessive rain, which could cause them to rot. A good rate of germination means that plants rapidly build up great colonies of tubers and can form quite dense groundcover.

CARING FOR PLANTS

When the leaves wither in early summer, add a mulch of leaf mold. New plants establish themselves more readily if they are bought and planted as growing plants.

Cyclamen hederifolium produces flowers before its leaves. For best results, plant it out when it is in full growth rather than as a dormant tuber.

70

Cytisus scoparius

Scotch broom

ZONE 5–9

This shrub is a common plant, native to western Europe. It has tough, wiry, green stems, and the leaves are reduced to tiny leaflets that are perfectly adapted to conserve water. By late spring it is smothered in pretty yellow flowers, similar in shape (but not size) to sweet peas. These are followed by typical pea pod seedcases, and on a hot day you can actually hear them popping as they burst open and scatter seeds.

Scotch broom is banned as a noxious plant in California, Hawaii, Idaho, Oregon, and Washington.

WHERE TO PLANT

Scotch broom grows to about 5ft (1.5m) high and makes a good shelter or specimen bush in difficult conditions. It grows naturally in hot, open sites where the ground is poor and baked dry in the summer, and it prefers free-draining, sandy soil that does not become waterlogged. The white-flowered Portuguese broom (*C. multiflorus*) tolerates similar conditions.

CARING FOR PLANTS

Brooms tend to be short-lived, and after about ten years they start to look straggly and leggy, so be prepared and have some replacement cuttings growing and waiting in the wings. The best time to take cuttings is late summer. Make sure you take them with a heel—a strip of the main stem to which they were attached—for best results.

Brooms do not really need pruning, but if you need to keep a bush in check, trim it back after flowering. Never cut into old wood because it will not regenerate.

The yellow, pealike flowers of Cytisus scoparius are carried in graceful arching sprays from late spring and on into summer.

Daphne laureola

Spurge laurel

ZONE
4–9

Spurge laurel has leathery, glossy, dark green leaves. In late winter and early spring it has clusters of greenish-yellow flowers, half hidden in the axils of the leaves. These have a sweet scent, which is most evident at night. The flowers are followed by small black fruits.

WHERE TO PLANT
Shade suits spurge laurel, and the shiny leaves reflect what little light there is in a gloomy corner. The soil can be anything from permanently damp to dry. This species makes a small, wide bush, about 3ft (1m) tall and up to 5ft (1.5m) across, and is useful for underplanting below taller shrubs or trees in a woodland setting.

CARING FOR PLANTS
Spurge laurels are not particularly long-lived shrubs, so it is wise to have some spares in reserve taken from cuttings in summer. Alternatively, look out for self-set seedlings. There's no need to prune, apart from taking out dead or spindly branches.

Spurge laurel is valued because it is evergreen and looks good all year round, forming a small, compact bush.

Dipsacus fullonum

Teasel

ZONE
4–10

From a flat rosette of bristly leaves, teasels send up great branched flowering stems with striking, egg-shaped flowerheads. Each flowerhead bristles with spines and is studded with hundred of tiny flowerlets, usually pale purple. Elegant, spiny bracts (a sort of narrow leaf) curl upward around the whole flowerhead. Bees find the flowers irresistible, and later on, once seed has set, seed-eating birds flock to the plants.

There is another species, *Dipsacus sativus*, which has larger flowerheads with paler flowers and more decorative bracts. It grows to the same height as *D. fullonum* and likes the same growing conditions.

The common teasel is banned as a noxious plant in Colorado, Iowa and New Mexico.

WHERE TO PLANT
Teasels are native to hedgerows, fields and banks on heavy clay soils. They also grow beside streams and are suitable for damp areas of the garden. They are biennials, so if you are sowing from seed, remember that plants will not mature and flower until the following year. Teasels are ideal for wildlife gardens and for bringing height and structure to any plot. It's best not to site them too close to a path or a children's play area because of their prickles.

CARING FOR PLANTS
Biennials usually die after flowering, but teasels are prolific self-seeders, so you shouldn't run short of plants. Teasel seedheads make popular dried flowers but take care when cutting them as they are seriously spiny.

Once they have finished flowering, teasels can be cut and dried for winter arrangements. In a wildlife garden flowerheads can be left on the plant to attract seed-eating birds.

Dryopteris filix-mas

Wood fern, shield fern, male fern

ZONE 1–9

The wood fern is the least fussy of all ferns and tolerates a wide range of conditions. This makes it one of the most versatile of foliage plants. It is semi-evergreen and looks good nearly all year round, although the old fronds do turn a little ratty before the new ones unfurl.

WHERE TO PLANT

Use the wood fern to bring life to dry, barren borders against a shady wall or to liven up the gloomy passage along the side of a typical house in older neighborhoods. Mimic its natural woodland habit and plant it under trees or tall shrubs.

CARING FOR PLANTS

In poor conditions—full shade with dry soil— improve the soil with leaf mold or well-rotted garden compost and water well before planting. Make sure that the fern gets enough water over the next few months, but once it's established it will not need any further help from you. Cut back the old fronds once the new ones emerge so that you can appreciate their beauty as they unfurl.

Give the wood fern a good start in an unpromising spot and it will rise to the challenge and brighten up a gloomy, dry corner.

Echinops ritro

Globe thistle

ZONE 3–10

Globe thistles are typical drought-resistant plants. They have narrowly divided, spiny leaves with silvery undersides that help to reduce moisture loss. The stems are silver-gray, too, and contrast with the steel blue flowerheads, which open in succession from midsummer to autumn. Globe thistles make good cut flowers and can be dried for winter arrangements.

WHERE TO PLANT

Globe thistles must have full sun to thrive and develop. Use them to stabilize a dry, sandy bank, where the basal rosette of leaves will help to resist soil erosion, or plant them to create shelter for smaller plants in an open, exposed garden.

CARING FOR PLANTS

All plants that are grown in tough conditions benefit from a little initial cosseting until they become established, and globe thistles are no exception. Once they have put down strong roots, however, there will be no stopping them. Globe thistles tolerate poor soils, so there is no need to add any well-rotted manure or garden compost, but if the soil is heavy, work in some gravel before planting, unless the site is on a hot, southfacing slope. Keep plants well watered in their first season; thereafter, they will be maintenance-free. Globe thistles soon form large clumps, which can be divided to give even more coverage.

Aphids can be persistent. If you do not want to use a chemical spray, diligently cut off the affected stems.

In silhouette the flowerheads of Echinops ritro are drumstick shaped. When they are in full bloom, each perfect globe is packed with tiny blue florets.

74

Elaeagnus pungens

Silverberry

ZONE
7–10

Silverberry is a large, evergreen shrub grown chiefly for its foliage. The leaves are basically dark green but with a curious metallic sheen on the upper surface and dull silver on the lower surface. There are several cultivars. 'Goldrim', as the name suggests, has dark green leaves with pronounced gold edges; the popular 'Maculata' has bold gold splashes on the leaves.

Although it is grown as a foliage plant, silverberry does flower in autumn. The flowers are tiny and hidden by the leaves, yet they smell sweetly and unless you know that silverberry is a fragrant shrub, it can be quite puzzling to work out where the perfume is coming from. Very occasionally, flowers go on to set fruit. The berries produced can be red, brown, or even silver.

76

WHERE TO PLANT
The shrub is not fussy about soil and is not damaged by strong winds, even salt-laden seaside gales. Use it as hedging, on its own or in a mixed hedge, or to create a windbreak. After some years it can get to 12ft (4m) high. Silverberry also tolerates partial shade, making the variegated cultivars useful for cheering up a dull corner, though the cultivars are less hardy than the species plant. Silverberry can also be grown in containers while small, as its evergreen foliage makes an attractive display all year round. Eventually, however, it will outgrow any pot unless rigorously pruned to keep it in shape.

CARING FOR PLANTS
Set out new plants of *E. pungens* in spring or wait until autumn before planting. Pruning shouldn't be necessary, except to keep shrubs in shape. If you plant variegated cultivars, cut out any shoots that revert to plain green so that the whole plant does not revert.

Elaeagnus pungens 'Maculata' has evergreen leaves splashed with gold. Be on the alert for any plain green leaves and prune them out as soon as they appear.

Enkianthus campanulatus

Red-vein enkianthus

| ZONE |
| 4–7 |

Enkianthus campanulatus is the hardiest species in this genus of shrubs from the Far East. It flowers in spring with pretty, pendulous, bell-shaped blooms, which may be cream, red, or pink, often with contrasting veining on the petals. In autumn, the dull green leaves change color to a breathtaking display of reds, yellows, and oranges.

WHERE TO PLANT
Enkianthus does best in moist acidic soil, although it will tolerate neutral soil, especially if lots of leaf mold is dug in before planting. It can put up with quite a bit of shade or will grow in full sun. What it does not like is strong winds. The shrubs are slow growing, reaching a mere 2–3ft (0.6–1m) after around five years, although eventually they can get to 10ft (3m), less tall in colder areas. Mix with other plants that thrive in acidic soil, such as rhododendrons, pieris and azaleas, for an interesting contrast of foliage.

CARING FOR PLANTS
Mulch with leaf mold in spring. Shrubs should not need pruning until they get old and straggly, when they can be cut back severely in spring, if necessary. The deeper the shade, the more slowly *E. campanulatus* will spread.

As it blooms on the previous year's wood, prune only to remove dead or damaged wood. If you wish to prune to shape the shrub, prune immediately after blooming has finished.

You can increase your stock of plants either by taking cuttings in summer or by layering older branches. This involves pegging the branches down into the soil so that roots form at the point of contact. It can take a year or so for roots to be produced. Then cut away the little plantlet and grow on in a pot for a while.

As a change from typical acid-loving rhododendrons and camellias, try planting Enkianthus campanulata *with its pretty bell-shaped flowers.*

77

Erica cinerea

Heath, bell heather

pH ZONE 5–9

Erica cinerea is one of hundreds of heathers that make undemanding plants once established. The species has spires of white, intense pink, or purple flowers in summer and autumn, and they contrast well with the deep green, evergreen leaves. Its spreading habit makes it a useful groundcover plant, although you may need to use a mulch, such as bark chippings, to keep weeds down until the plants spread.

WHERE TO PLANT
Plant heathers out in the open, away from deciduous trees because dead autumn leaves snagged in among the heather can appear quite messy, especially as *E. cinerea* is an autumn-flowering species. An exposed windy site is fine—just imagine the windswept moors where they grow naturally—but heathers must have acidic soil.

CARING FOR PLANTS
Set out new plants in late fall, if possible when the soil is still warm. Water plants in hot spells for the first year or two, and they will develop far-reaching, healthy root systems that spare you the trouble of further nurturing in years to come. Clip lightly after flowering to maintain plants in good, compact shape.

Erica cinerea 'Pink Ice' is one of the smaller cultivars suitable for acid soil and exposed sites, growing to just 8in (20cm) tall.

78

Eryngium bourgatii

Sea holly

ZONE
5–9

The thistlelike flowerheads of sea holly are produced in summer, and are studded with tiny blue flowers that match the plant's unusual blue stems. Shields of spiny bracts radiate from the flowerheads.

The flowers are especially attractive to bees, and as they age their color changes in intensity from steely blue to a paler lavender blue.

WHERE TO PLANT
E. bourgatii is well adapted to thrive in hot, dry gardens. It doesn't mind sandy soils, and its tough, silver-green leaves resist the drying action of winds. Sea holly plants should reach at least 18in (45cm) tall when in flower and spread to make a good-sized clump—another wind- and drought-resistant feature of plants that have adapted to tough conditions.

CARING FOR PLANTS
Eryngiums must have well-drained soil or they can be prone to rot in wet winters. In a prolonged cold, wet spell it is worth clearing away any dead leaves from the base of the plant to prevent moisture lingering and rot setting in. They do best in poor soil: rich soil promotes soft, floppy growth.

Eryngium bourgatii *is worth growing for its foliage alone. The leaves are deeply fretted and highlighted with silver veining.*

79

Escallonia 'Donard Seedling'

Escallonia

Escallonias are generally evergreen, with glossy leaves and small but pretty clusters of pink or red flowers throughout summer and on into autumn. 'Donard Seedling', one of the taller cultivars, grows eventually to about 10ft (3m). There is a wide range of cultivars, but some are slightly tender, so choose one of the more vigorous ones for an exposed garden.

WHERE TO PLANT

Escallonias not only survive strong winds unshaken but can also tolerate salt-laden gales along coasts. For this reason they make excellent hedging for exposed gardens and provide valuable shelter for less tolerant plants.

CARING FOR PLANTS

Severe weather in spring can be a setback when the plants are putting on new growth, but the hardier escallonias are usually tough enough to fight back. Any dieback simply acts as a sort of natural pruning and the plants swiftly recover. Pruning is necessary only to remove unsightly scorching or to reshape an unruly shrub.

The flowers of Escallonia 'Donard Seedling' are borne all summer long, making it good value in an exposed garden.

Eschscholzia californica

California poppy

These poppies, the state flower of California, have the typical gray-green leaves of a sun-tolerant plant. The papery petals of the flowers come in shades of orange, yellow, and cream. The elongated buds are like neatly furled umbrellas until they open. Once fully open, the blooms have the habit of closing up on cloudy days. Despite producing flowers in profusion, they do not make good cut flowers because the petals drop too quickly.

WHERE TO PLANT

Do not pamper California poppies. If you consider that they grow wild in large numbers in the Californian grasslands and on roadsides, you'll understand why they need poor soil and hot, sunny conditions to flower well. In colder regions they are grown as annuals. Sow the seed straight in the ground where you want them. A spring sowing will produce plants that flower later that summer; with an autumn sowing, plants will have a head start for flowering in early summer the following year. In warmer areas, they self-seed freely

CARING FOR PLANTS

Deadheading plants prolongs the flowering period, but if you leave some seed pods to ripen, California poppies often self-seed, saving you the bother of repeat sowings each year. Do not try to shift self-set seedlings to a different position, however, because the resulting root disturbance usually affects plants adversely.

The original California poppies have orange flowers, but plant breeding programs have introduced a range of new colors, including pink.

Euonymus fortunei 'Emerald 'n' Gold'

Wintercreeper

No one grows euonymus for the flowers; the foliage is everything. 'Emerald 'n' Gold' has butter-yellow leaves with a central splash of strong green; in winter the leaves develop a pink edging. 'Emerald Gaiety' has white-edged leaves that turn bronze in the fall.

WHERE TO PLANT
Use 'Emerald 'n' Gold' to cheer up barren, shady borders along the side of a house or garage. Although it will climb, you could train it up (or down) to cover a steep, shady slope. It grows well in chalk soils, and in heavy clay to a slightly lesser extent.

CARING FOR PLANTS
Pruning is not strictly necessary, although older, untidy plants do respond well to being cut back hard at any time of the year except spring. If any stems of variegated cultivars revert to green, cut them out immediately.

The foliage plant Euonymus fortunei *'Emerald 'n' Gold' grows well in shade and tolerates a range of soil types.*

Filipendula ulmaria

Meadowsweet, queen of the meadow

Meadowsweet, a familiar wildflower of damp meadows and ditches with its froth of creamy, sweet-smelling plumes in summer, has also been bred for the garden. *Filipendula ulmaria* 'Rosea' has pale pink flowers, and 'Variegata' has yellow-variegated leaves. The plants have blood-red stalks that contrast with the ribbed, almost pleated green leaves.

Two other vigorous species enjoy similar conditions. *F. purpurea* has plumes of purplish flowers. *F. rubra* 'Venusta' has deep pink flowers and grows to about 6ft (2m) tall.

WHERE TO PLANT
Match meadowsweet's natural habitat and use it to plant up permanently wet patches in the garden, especially areas in semi-shade. It suits damp ditches and swales and will grow in the wet margins of ponds. All plants reach at least 4ft (1.2m), so do not completely encircle a pond with them or you will never get near it. Avoid harsh, sunny conditions.

CARING FOR PLANTS
Set plants out in late winter or spring. Overgrown clumps can be divided at the same time of year. If the foliage gets unsightly toward the end of the year, cut back plants to ground level.

Some gardeners grow meadowsweet for its foliage alone and will snip off flowers to avoid detracting from the leaves— especially with 'Variegata'. This practice also ensures the plant uses its energy to produce perfect leaves, not flowers.

The pleated leaves of meadowsweet with their contrasting red stems need a permanently wet or boggy site in the garden.

Fuchsia magellanica

Magellan fuchsia

ZONE
6–9

There are hundreds of cultivars of fuchsia with elaborate frilled flowers in extraordinary color combinations, but for tough hedging and windbreaks it is the hardy species, *F. magellanica* that should be chosen. It has classic, pendent flowers in a rather ecclesiastical combination of purple and red, and the flowers are followed by small, sausage-shaped fruits that are eggplant in color and in miniature shape, too.

WHERE TO PLANT

Hardy fuchsias grow wild on the mild English coastlines, rearing up into great shaggy hedges and dwarfing low cottages tucked into the landscape. In the garden they make effective windbreaks and attractive informal hedges. In mild areas this species may remain green all winter long, but even when it loses its leaves the twiggy framework still filters strong winds.

CARING FOR PLANTS

Cut back new plants to about 1ft (30cm) before their first winter. This will stop the wind from rocking the plants and unsettling new root systems. If you have planted fuchsias late in the summer, give them a little frost protection—woodchips or newspaper tucked around the stems—because hardy fuchsias are only truly hardy if they have been in the ground since early summer. Even though all growth above ground will be killed by a severe winter, this species will grow back quickly from the base. In colder areas, the base of the plant will need added winter protection.

The sausage-shaped fruits that follow the elegant flowers of the Magellan fuchsia are edible and were once used to make jam.

84

Galium odoratum

Sweet woodruff

ZONE
5–10

In late spring, sweet woodruff forms a carpet of starry, white flowers in the most unpromising situations. It is low growing, with leaves in a fresh shade of green, arranged around the stem in ruffs (technically whorls). A handful of stems makes a pretty little bouquet, and it is such a prolific plant that cut stems often root in the vase. The flowers are scentless, but if the whole plant is dried, it develops the smell of new-mown hay. The closely related species *G. mollugo* is a scrambling plant that can be useful for covering up bare rose stems or scrambling through shrubs in general.

WHERE TO PLANT

Sweet woodruff will grow just about anywhere, making it the perfect plant for awkward, dry, shady spots below shallow-rooted trees, such as silver birch and Norway maple, or for lightening the area at ground level under a mass of shrubs. It is an effective groundcover plant—rather too effective, you may find, if it escapes into sunnier spots with richer soil where it can become quite rampant and may smother neighboring small plants. Sweet woodruff spreads rapidly but can be divided in fall or spring if desired.

CARING FOR PLANTS

Plants need minimal attention. Sometimes they will look neater if the old leaves are clipped off at the end of winter but be careful to avoid damaging new shoots as they emerge.

There is something very fresh about the combination of sweet woodruff's pure brilliant white flowers and the particular shade of green of its leaves.

85

Geranium macrorrhizum

Bigroot geranium, scented cranesbill

These geraniums are not the tender container plants, which are actually pelargoniums, but are hardy perennials that do well in sun or shade.

Soft, downy leaves and purplish, pale pink or white flowers characterize this hardy geranium. It flowers in spring, and when the petals drop the developing seedheads still have a certain charm. They have a bulbous base and a long pointed "beak," hence the common name, cranesbill, for this type of geranium. The leaves are strong-smelling, having a vaguely antiseptic scent, mixed with a hint of cat urine, but surprisingly not entirely unpleasant.

WHERE TO PLANT

G. macrorrhizum thrives in poor, dry soil in shade, vigorously growing to form an attractive clump. Plants also self-seed to make a spreading groundcover colony. In heavier shade, the much paler flowers of the cultivar *G. macrorrhizum* 'Album' will lighten the gloom. In warmer areas, plants keep their leaves all year round and the old foliage often turns color in autumn, typically to rusty red. They are also worth growing in containers in shade.

CARING FOR PLANTS

Cut off the seedheads if you do not want more seedlings. Any bare, trailing stems can be cut back to promote new growth, but generally these plants are trouble-free.

Along with the clear pink flowers of Geranium macrorrhizum, the first few flowers that have gone to seed are visible—they are just starting to develop the typical long, pointed, cranesbill shape.

Gypsophila paniculata

Baby's breath

Fleshy, gray-green leaves give a clue to how this favorite of florists tolerates full sun. In summer it sends up sprays of simple white flowers, sometimes veined with pink. Baby's breath can also be cut and dried for long-lasting arrangements.

WHERE TO PLANT

Baby's breath is tough enough to take full sun in a dry, free-draining sandy soil. In flower the plants can get to 4ft (1.2m) tall. Use them to create an airy cloud of blossom that links and interweaves among stronger flowers, such as poppies. Look out for other cultivars, which include the double, pale pink-flowered 'Flamingo' and 'Schneeflocke', which has double, white flowers.

Baby's breath is banned as a noxious plant in California, Manitoba and Washington.

CARING FOR PLANTS

Picking flowers regularly encourages plants to carry on blooming well into autumn. Set out new plants in spring and at the same time push in some canes or twiggy sticks to support the plants as they come into flower.

87

Baby's breath in flower is a cloud of white, stunning on its own as here or mixed in with stronger colors. This cultivar is 'Bristol Fairy'.

Hebe albicans

Hebe

ZONE
8–10

Hebe albicans is a pretty, fairly low-growing shrub that seldom exceeds 3ft (1m). It makes a satisfying dome shape as it grows. The small, gray-green, oval leaves are thick and fleshy in appearance, and small spires of white flowers are produced in late spring and summer.

WHERE TO PLANT

This hebe does well in most soils and is particularly useful in sandy or chalky soil. The grayish foliage helps it stand up to full sun, and its compact dome shape survives in coastal sites, where it is exposed to salt-laden winds. Most hebes do well in similar situations, and the genus is large so you can choose from taller species, which are ideal for hedging, to smaller plants, which will grow in containers. One thing

to watch out for is hardiness, because although *H. albicans* is completely hardy to zone 8, some species are relatively tender.

CARING FOR PLANTS

Set out new plants in autumn or spring. Old bushes that have become unsightly and straggly can be cut back hard in spring, but do not go too far. Leave some older branches to help start the shrub back into life. These can be cut out the following spring.

Hebes quickly grow to their full size: in the case of compactly rounded Hebe albicans *this is a maximum of around 3ft (1m).*

Hedera helix

English ivy

ZONE
3–10

Ivy hardly needs any introduction. The glossy, evergreen leaves look good all year round, and although the flowers are hardly spectacular, they are an important source of nectar for bees and many other insects. The berries that follow are popular with birds and also provide winter color. *Hedera helix* is the species from which many cultivars have been developed, including 'Glacier', which has gray and cream variegated leaves. The naturally occurring *H. helix* f. *poetarium*, which is sometimes known as poet's ivy, has yellow berries and glossy, dark green leaves. Some of the cultivars, however, are not as hardy and are used as houseplants in colder regions, so choose carefully for garden use.

WHERE TO PLANT
Plant ivy where it seems nothing else will grow. Use it as groundcover in the dense, dry shade cast by evergreen trees; squeeze it in where tree roots form an impenetrable layer just below the soil surface; or train it up a cold sunless wall.

Some species, such as *H. colchica* (Persian ivy), which has large, yellow-splashed leaves, and *H. hibernica* (Irish ivy), are self-clinging and do not need a support system put in place on a wall.

CARING FOR PLANTS
Ivies are generally so vigorous that they can be cut back at any time of year if they start to overstep their limits. Sometimes the variegated varieties become less well-marked in heavy shade, and soil that is too fertile can sometimes have the same effect.

Hedera helix 'Goldchild' is a popular plant for containers. When new, the leaves are a combination of pale green and yellow. As they mature they turn gray-green with cream-colored margins.

89

Helenium 'Moerheim Beauty'

Sneezeweed

ZONE 5–9

The rich coppery red flowers of *Helenium* 'Moerheim Beauty' will set a border ablaze. They are daisy-shaped with dark brown centers raised up into a central boss set above a mass of midgreen leaves. Look for 'Wyndley', which has the same velvety dark brown centers to its flowers, but its yellow petals are splashed with orange.

WHERE TO PLANT

These are plants of the North American prairies. They tolerate heavy clay without giving up and also do well on thin, chalky soil. Put them in full sun, and they will reward you with masses of flowers from early summer to early autumn. The average height is 3ft (1m), making them ideal mid-border plants.

CARING FOR PLANTS

When planting new plants, put in some stakes or twiggy sticks to support the flowers. Regular deadheading will prolong the flowering season and boost the number of flowers produced. After two or three years clumps can become congested and will not flower so well. Divide and replant to revitalize them.

The flowers of Helenium 'Moerheim Beauty' *are a bonus in autumn when many other species are past their best.*

Hippophae rhamnoides

Sea buckthorn

ZONE 2–9

Sea buckthorn is native to large areas in Europe and temperate Asia, and it has made its way into the gardener's repertoire because of its resilience to harsh conditions. The linear leaves are covered in silvery scales for protection against sun scorch and water loss. Female and male flowers are borne on different plants, and to be sure of a crop of orange autumn berries, you need to plant one male bush with several females.

WHERE TO PLANT

In the wild, sea buckthorn grows on hot, dry, free-draining sand dunes. In the garden give it the hottest, driest site you can. Its tough nature makes it an ideal shrub for coastal gardens, and its thorniness makes it a useful hedge. It grows to around 10ft (3m) tall, producing a tangled mass of branches that just keep on spreading. Although the shrub is deciduous, it is so densely branched that it makes an excellent windbreak even in winter.

CARING FOR PLANTS

If you need to reshape a bush or are using sea buckthorn in a more formal hedge, do this in summer, but otherwise pruning shouldn't be necessary.

The almost impenetrable tracery of branches of **Hippophae rhamnoides** *illustrates its excellent properties as a windbreak.*

Hosta 'Big Daddy'

Plantain lily

| | | pH | ZONE 6–10 |

This hosta is a bit of a heavyweight, as its name suggests. It is one of the tougher, larger cultivars—to 2ft (60cm) tall and 3ft (1m) across—and has leaves puckered like seersucker, with a true blue sheen. The flowers are pale, somewhere between violet and white, and are produced in summer.

WHERE TO PLANT

Hostas prefer shade—bright sun can scorch their large, thin leaves—but it has to be *moist* shade. The density of the shade has a bearing on how prolifically they flower. In near-permanent shade you may have to appreciate them more for their beautiful foliage than for their flowers. But they are exceedingly useful plants for the shade garden and indispensable in deep shade. Some can reach enormous, almost prehistoric-looking sizes. They tolerate slightly acidic to neutral soils.

CARING FOR PLANTS

Before planting a hosta in heavy clay, work in a spadeful of gravel or grit in the bottom of the planting hole to help with drainage. Mulch plants in autumn with well-rotted manure or garden compost. Be diligent against slugs and snails, which can devastate tender new growth. A slug trap or saucer of beer nearby will help cut down on these pests, as will inspecting plants regularly, particularly during a rainy spell.

The extraordinary blue-green leaves of Hosta 'Big Daddy' with their intricate puckering and veining are justification enough for growing the plant, whether you manage to coax it to flower or not.

Hydrangea anomola subsp. petiolaris

Climbing hydrangea

| | | | ZONE 2–11 |

This climbing plant has the typical flowerheads of a lacecap hydrangea. In the right circumstances, it may seem like the sky's the limit as it scrambles skyward—monsters of up to 40ft (12m) have been recorded. They can also spread the same distance horizontally. Remember, though, that they flower more where they get the most light, so if your hydrangea climbs too high, you may miss out on its beautiful blooms at the top.

WHERE TO PLANT

The climbing hydrangea is self-clinging and needs no extra support to scale walls, fences and even poles. It is ideal for gloomy alleys between houses, where its frothy white flowers lighten a shady wall in summer.

CARING FOR PLANTS

In dry summers, flowers do not last very long, so give plants a good drenching to keep the flowers from fading too quickly. If you give this hydrangea enough space, you shouldn't need to prune it, apart from cutting out the odd awkwardly placed branch after flowering.

As long as the light levels are adequate, the climbing hydrangea will bloom prolifically with typical lacecap-style flowerheads.

93

Hypericum calycinum

St. John's wort

| | | | | ZONE 3–9 |

The bright yellow, cup-shaped flowers of St. John's wort are borne for a long period, starting at the beginning of summer and carrying on well into autumn. There are other species of hypericum, but *H. calycinum* is one of the hardiest, along with *H. androsaemum*, which has smaller flowers and is deciduous.

WHERE TO PLANT
St. John's wort is a useful groundcover species. Plant it to form a lowish carpet, with a maximum height of 2ft (60cm), below taller shrubs or under trees in a woodland setting. You can grow it as groundcover in the sun, too, where it will flower more prolifically.

CARING FOR PLANTS
Deadheading can help to prolong flowering. For vigorous, bushy growth, trim back plants in spring to create a neat shape. Older specimens benefit from being cut back hard to the ground at the same time of year, which will rejuvenate them. In a particularly cold winter, plants of *H. calycinum* may lose their leaves.

The flowers of Hypericum calycinum *are cup-shaped and bright yellow with a delicate central tassel of stamens.*

94

Kalmia latifolia

Calico bush, mountain laurel

| | | | pH | ZONE 3–9 |

The flower buds of the calico bush look like perfect pink cake decorations, and when they open they retain a curious crimped appearance. The bush flowers in late spring and early summer, and for the rest of the year it is a handsome evergreen, densely packed with glossy, oval leaves.

WHERE TO PLANT
The calico bush makes an interesting companion to rhododendrons in acidic soil. Plant it in a woodland setting under taller trees—it grows to a maximum 10ft (3m)— where it will do well in the shade. It is equally at home in sun and, as is usual with many flowering shrubs, will flower more freely the sunnier its position is. Do not put it in a spot where the soil will dry out because it needs a permanently moist position.

CARING FOR PLANTS
Deadhead regularly to keep the bush looking good while it is in flower. Pruning shouldn't be necessary, but if the shrub gets out of shape or there are one or two rogue branches cut these out in spring. The calico bush flowers on the previous year's wood, so any pruning must be done straight after flowering. Do not be impatient with a small new bush: it may take a few years to flower.

'Ostbo Red' is the most widely grown cultivar of Kalmia latifolia, *the calico bush. It has red buds that open to reveal pink flowers.*

Kirengeshoma palmata

Yellow wax bells

ZONE 5–10

The species is an unusual and elegant plant from the Far East. It has lobed leaves, rather like an oriental maple, and in late summer it sends up spires of creamy-white flowers, each with a neatly contrasting dark brown calyx capping the petals. Plants can vary considerably in height, ranging from 2 to 4ft (0.6–1.2m).

WHERE TO PLANT

In its native habitat in Japan, *Kirengeshoma palmata* is a tough perennial woodland plant and can be used to underplant shrubs and trees where the soil is moist. It will not suit sites that dry out in summer.

It prefers acidic soil but may cope in neutral conditions if other factors are favorable and plenty of leaf mold is worked into the soil before planting.

CARING FOR PLANTS

If plants show signs of flagging in dry spells, water them thoroughly. A mulch of garden compost or leaf mold will help to conserve moisture. Mulch soil only after heavy rain, otherwise a thick layer may prevent water from reaching the plant's roots.

Kirengeshoma palmata is an unusual species for shade. Plant it in a moist, shady corner and visitors are sure to ask you what it is.

Kniphofia caulescens

Red-hot poker, torch lily, poker plant

ZONE 6–9

Great, knotted, knobby stems of red-hot pokers lie along the ground and send up exotic rosettes of gray-green leaves. They flower late in summer and on into autumn. The flower stems gave rise to their common name: the newest florets at the top of spikes are an intense red as they open, fading to yellow further down the flower spike as they age.

WHERE TO PLANT

Choose a spot in full sunshine in fairly poor soil. Set them at the back of a border, not only because of their height, which can top 3½ft (1.1m) or more, but also to draw attention away from their rather unprepossessing appearance earlier in the year.

There are about 70 species of red-hot poker, but *K. caulescens* is the only truly hardy one. If your garden is cold, it's probably a waste of time experimenting with others. But if you live on a coast or have a sheltered garden in a city, other species or cultivars may be worth a try, such as 'Earliest of All', 'Glow', 'Gold Mine', 'Parmientier', 'Primrose Mascot', 'Shenanddoah', 'Springtime', 'Vanilla', 'Wayside Flame' or 'White Fairy'. *K. uvaria* is another hardy species with bright red flowers. When the foliage dies back, add a protective winter mulch to help it survive freezing temperatures.

CARING FOR PLANTS

If an exceptionally cold spell is forecast in winter it may be wise to add a layer of branches, wood chips, or newspaper to protect overwintering plants. For best results, get new plants in the garden in early autumn or wait until spring.

The great shaggy flowerheads of Kniphofia caulescens, pointing skyward, set the border on fire in autumn.

Lamium maculatum

Dead nettle, spotted nettle

ZONE
4–10

Lamium maculatum is closely related to its wild cousin *L. purpureum*. It has typical dead nettle flowers with an upper and lower lip, toothed nettlelike leaves, and square stalks. It's odd how some regard one as a weed and the other as something to pay for. It does have a few added extras, such as bigger flowers and attractive silver stripes on its leaves. Other cultivars that have been developed include 'Silver Nancy', which has leaves that are almost pure silver with a frill of green and white flowers, and 'Aureum', which has white-splashed, gold leaves, and pink flowers.

WHERE TO PLANT

This dead nettle makes good groundcover in both full shade and areas that receive some sun during the day. It spreads quickly and makes a dense carpet of leaves. It doesn't mind alkaline or chalky soil, but it is vital that soil is free-draining.

CARING FOR PLANTS

Cut back after flowering to encourage a fresh burst of weed-smothering growth. Beware of siting it too close to more retiring species—it is no respecter of the difference between weeds and garden plants and will overtake anything in its way. Cultivars are less vigorous.

An ideal groundcover plant, Lamium maculatum *will thrive in a wide range of conditions, including both sun and shade.*

98

Lathyrus rotundifolius

Sweet pea

ZONE
1–10

The sweet pea has typical pealike flowers in an intense shade of purplish-pink, crammed onto long flowering stalks in summer. The leaves are dark green. It is a tough and vigorous climber. More familiar is the perennial sweet pea (*Lathyrus latifolius*), which has slightly larger flowers, purple rather than pink, and which are produced until well into autumn. It also has curious "winged" stems with a thin, leafy flange on each side. Both species are tough, prolific climbers.

WHERE TO PLANT
Sweet pea absolutely prefers shade to sun. Grow it against a wall or fence with trellis or netting for support because it is not self-clinging. The more common perennial sweet pea is slightly more versatile in that it will grow happily in sun or shade and can also be left to grow as groundcover or on banks and slopes, or even horizontally.

CARING FOR PLANTS
Pinch out the tips of plants in spring to encourage a thick, bushy shape. Keep deadheading flowers to prolong the display or cut them for the house for a short-lived bouquet—the color quickly fades in water. Cut plants right back to ground level in autumn if you like to keep your garden tidy or wait until spring.

The flowering stems of Lathyrus rotundifolius *are crammed with blooms.*

99

Lavandula angustifolia

Lavender

ZONE 4–10

Lavender deserves a place in every garden with a hot, sunny space to fill, and the late-summer flowers are a favorite with gardeners, bees, and butterflies alike. The narrow, gray-green foliage and the fragrant volatile oils it releases indicate that this is a plant well adapted to dry soil in full sun. Its dried flowers have been popular for centuries; for best drying results cut them before the buds are fully open.

WHERE TO PLANT
Plant lavender as a low-growing hedge, to 2ft (60cm) tall, to separate areas of a garden or to edge a path or patio. Put it somewhere you visit regularly so that you can appreciate its fragrance as you pass. Like many aromatic Mediterranean plants, lavender is ideal for hot, dry sites, and it must have full sun to flourish. It does not like winter wet and cold, so soil must be free-draining to avoid roots rotting.

CARING FOR PLANTS
Once the flowers have finished cut back the spent stems in autumn. At the same time lightly clip the foliage with shears. Leave any serious pruning until spring, because the resulting new shoots are easily damaged by frost. When reshaping an old bush, never cut into the old wood, because it is highly unlikely to regenerate. Ultimately, it's better to dig out an old shrub that's past its prime and replant with a new one.

'Munstead' is one of a range of cultivars of Lavandula angustifolia. It has short flower spikes and grayish-green leaves.

Ligularia macrophylla

Ligularia

ZONE 3–9

The yellow, daisylike flowers of *Ligularia macrophylla* are massed together on tall spires. The flowering stems can reach 5ft (1.5m) and make a bold planting in midsummer. Equally prominent are its leaves: gray-green and roughly oval, they can be to 2ft (60cm) long.

WHERE TO PLANT
Ligularia is a waterside plant, growing best when its roots are in soil that is permanently wet. Plant in the boggy margins of a pond where it can tolerate a little sun. Alternatively, chose a site that is moist rather than wet, but make sure the spot is permanently shady. Give it plenty of room to show off its huge, handsome leaves.

CARING FOR PLANTS
In an exposed garden the flower stems may need staking. Strong winds can also cause the leaves to wilt. Give plants a thick mulch every spring with well-rotted garden compost.

The flowers of Ligularia 'Gregynog Gold' are orange-gold. This cultivar can stand more sun than most.

Limonium platyphyllum

Sea lavender, statice

The tough, wiry stems and leathery leaves of sea lavender are typical of a plant evolved to withstand difficult coastal conditions. The leaves are arranged in a rosette, which helps to conserve moisture and stabilize the soil. In summer and autumn statice is a haze of tiny, pale lavender flowers which are a rich source of nectar for bees and butterflies.

WHERE TO PLANT
In a seaside garden, plant sea lavender in borders or alongside paths, wherever you like. Inland, plant it in gravel beds or in hot, open spaces baked by the sun. Take advantage of its airy flowerheads to create a pale purple cloud that will be a foil for bolder blooms.

CARING FOR PLANTS
Set out new plants in spring. Deadhead flowers to keep plants blooming or simply cut stems for the house. Cut out all flowering stems once the plant has finished flowering.

It's practically impossible to tell the difference between the fresh and dried flowerheads of sea lavender, but they look good in the border or a vase.

Lonicera sempervirens

Trumpet honeysuckle, coral honeysuckle

One of the longest-flowering honeysuckle species, trumpet honeysuckle is in bloom from spring until autumn. Its clusters of striking, red, tubular flowers, which give rise to its common name, gain extra emphasis from the leaves, which completely encircle the stem and the flowerhead like a chic, green frill of wrapping paper. The technical term for this type of leaf is perfoliate. From late summer onward, trumpet honeysuckle produces big, scarlet berries.

WHERE TO PLANT
Trumpet honeysuckle flowers better and more reliably in shade, so set the plant against a wall that is shaded for most of the day. Honeysuckles climb by twining and need some trellis tacked onto a wall or a system of horizontal wires to help them scramble up to cover a bare wall.

CARING FOR PLANTS
Trumpet honeysuckle is particularly susceptible to aphid attacks, though planting in shade helps to reduce the severity of any infestation. It shouldn't really need pruning, but spindly, damaged, or weak stems can be cut out in autumn. If your garden is in a particularly cold area, however, it may be wiser to leave this until spring.

The trumpet honeysuckle is a semi-evergreen climber, losing its circular leaves only in a bad winter. Large red berries follow the flowers.

Mahonia aquifolium

Oregon grapeholly

ZONE 5–10

Oregon grapeholly has glossy, dark green leaves with spiny, serrated margins, rather like a holly leaf, thus its common name. As winter sets in, the leaves turn a subtle shade of purplish-brown. At the same time, tantalizing clusters of flower buds appear, but the shrub doesn't properly burst into bloom until late spring. When the flowers finally open, you will certainly know, as they have a delicate lily-of-the-valley scent.

WHERE TO PLANT
The Oregon grapeholly is a versatile shrub, that can cope with a surprising range of conditions, from clay to sandy or chalky soil and from sun to shade, without showing any effect on flowers, foliage or growth. The species *M. aquifolium* forms a bush eventually 5ft (1.5m) tall, but there are several lower growing cultivars that make good groundcover plants. 'Apollo' reaches no more than 2ft (60cm) tall and often produces black berries after flowering. 'Smaragd' is similar but does not like sun.

CARING FOR PLANTS
Grow a mahonia as a feature shrub and it will not need pruning, apart from taking out the odd badly placed branch or straggly growth in either autumn or spring. It is prone to suckering, so if you want to keep a neat shape, the suckers can be dug up and replanted elsewhere or simply pulled out and composted. The two low-growing cultivars need to be sheared off at ground level every two or three years if you are using them as groundcover. Ideally, do this after they have flowered.

The tightly buttoned flower buds of the Oregon grapeholly stay firmly furled shut all through winter, until the temperature rises in spring.

Malus floribunda

Japanese flowering crabapple

ZONE 4–9

In spring the Japanese flowering crabapple tree is a mass of deep pink buds that open to reveal pale pink or even white petals. The genus *Malus* includes the domestic eating and cooking apples, and Japanese flowering crabapples produce fruits, too. The cultivar *M.* 'Evereste' has reddish-orange fruits instead of the yellow fruits of the species.

Other cultivars to try include 'Harvest Gold', which is particularly disease resistant, as is 'Prairie Fire' with maroon leaves and fruit that lasts well. 'Red Jade' is another crabapple that holds on to its fruit and has an attractive weeping habit, while 'Robinson' has pretty copper foliage. *M. toringo* subsp. *sargentii* (sometimes referred to as *M. sargentii*) is another disease-resistant form.

WHERE TO PLANT

While the Japanese flowering crabapple is an undemanding tree that tolerates chalk and clay— provided the ground is not permanently waterlogged—give some thought to where you place it. Although it stays a relatively small tree for many years, ultimately its canopy can be as wide as the tree is tall, which is quite some feat when you consider it may reach 20ft (6m) or more.

CARING FOR PLANTS

Shape the crown of the tree while it is small and the resulting mature tree should need little or no pruning. Simply take out any dead branches in winter. Although these trees are generally trouble free, they can succumb to honey fungus or fireblight, so keep an eye on them if these diseases have been noted in your neighborhood.

When mature, crabapple trees are often as wide as they are tall, as illustrated by this mature specimen of 'Evereste' in full bloom.

105

Molinia caerulea subsp. caerulea

Purple moor grass

ZONE
2–9

Ornamental grasses serve quite a different purpose from the turf you sow to make a lawn. Just like a flowering plant, moor grasses contribute delicate flowers and valuable autumn color to the garden. *Molinia caerulea* subsp. *caerulea*, one of the lower growing species of moor grass, grows to form clumps a manageable 3ft (1m) high. It has typical, grasslike, purple flowers in late summer, and the leaves turn butter yellow in the autumn. There are many cultivars, including 'Moorhexe', which is slightly smaller, and 'Moorflamme', which is the deepest purple of all.

WHERE TO PLANT
As its name indicates, purple moor grass is a moorland plant, native to acidic peat bogs, so plant it in any acidic, permanently boggy ground. It will also do well in merely damp soil, as long as it doesn't dry out. As it is a plant of open, exposed sites, it can also tolerate full sun.

CARING FOR PLANTS
Molinia is one of the few ornamental grasses that can be slow to establish. One way around this is to start off with the largest plants you can afford to buy. It's also unusual in that its leaves become detached and blow away in autumn—most deciduous grasses need a sharp tug to detach dead leaves.

Grasses have become popular garden plants and molinia is a species for a damp garden rather than a prairie-style planting. 'Edith Dudszus' produces rich purple flower spikelets.

Nepeta x faassenii

Catmint

ZONE
1–10

The wrinkled, greenish-gray leaves of catmint are covered with soft hairs—a defense against drought—and are also strongly aromatic. Cats love the smell, thus its common name, although generally they prefer catnip, *Nepeta cataria*, to *N. x faassenii*. Its pale purplish-blue flowers are arranged in spikes to 18in (45cm) tall. The cultivar *N.* 'Six Hill's Giant' has deeper purple flowers and grows to 3ft (1m) tall.

WHERE TO PLANT
Catmint is a deceptively pretty plant that is also a tough customer. It likes hot, dry sites and free-draining sandy or chalky soils, but will also grow in clay. It forms dense clumps that make a weed-suppressing groundcover.

CARING FOR PLANTS
Cutting back flowering stems once they're finished often stimulates another flush of blooms. Clip the whole plant lightly at the same time if growing it for groundcover. In spring cut out any old woody stems to rejuvenate plants.

107

The small, tubular flowers of Nepeta x faassenii *are clustered tightly all up the stems, and the plant has a relaxed spreading habit.*

Onoropordum acanthium

Scotch thistle, cotton thistle

ZONE
6–10

A colossal ornamental Scotch thistle in full flower and leaf is an arresting sight. Getting close to 8ft (2.4m) tall and around 3ft (1m) across, it produces typical thistle-type flowerheads, which are quite modest in size by comparison to the plant's overall size. Scotch thistles are packed with rich purple florets. Everything about the plant is spiny, from its silvery leaves to its "winged" stems.

WHERE TO PLANT
Scotch thistle is at home in dry gravel beds and hot, sunny borders. For obvious reasons, give it plenty of space and do not site it close to a path. Similarly, Scotch thistles and small children do not go together. Wait until the children are old enough to give it a wide berth before you try growing this spiny plant.

Scotch thistle is banned as a noxious plant in Arizona, British Columbia, California, Colorado, Idaho, Missouri, New Mexico, Nevada, Ontario, Oregon, Utah, Washington and Wyoming.

CARING FOR PLANTS
Scotch thistles are biennials, so for the first year of life they simply form a flat rosette of prickly leaves. For best results, set plants out at the end of summer or beginning of autumn for flowering the following summer. Cut off most of the seedheads to avoid seedlings springing up, but leave a few if you want more plants for subsequent years. Alternatively, try cutting the flowers for drying.

Scotch thistle has the silver leaves typical of a sun-loving plant. Silver foliage reflects the sun's rays.

Pachysandra terminalis

Japanese spurge

ZONE 1–10

Japanese spurge has oval, glossy, dark green leaves grouped together at the tops of its stems. In summer it bears small spikes of fragrant, white flowers, which are sometimes followed by white berries. There is also a variegated form, 'Variegata', with off-white edging to its leaves.

WHERE TO PLANT

Japanese spurge never grows taller than around 8in (20cm). Its height, combined with its free-spreading habit, makes it ideal for groundcover, and the stems root at intervals as they spread across the soil. It's an ideal shade plant, although the denser the shade, the more slowly it grows, but it will get there in the end. You may even consider mixing it with another groundcover plant, such as violets, until it fills in. Conversely, don't let it spread into areas of good soil or you may find yourself with an unstoppable invader on your hands.

CARING FOR PLANTS

Work in some leaf mold before setting plants out in early spring, especially if the soil is dry. Try not to let plants dry out in their first year or two—thereafter they should cope with all but the worst conditions.

Its habit of rooting at intervals makes cuttings easy to take and you can quickly increase your stock of plants.

Japanese spurge is a valuable plant in shade, where it will spread slowly to cover the ground.

109

Papaver rhoeas

Flanders field poppy, Shirley poppy

ZONE 5–9

The original Flanders field poppy typically has red petals with a black splash at the base of each. Occasionally the flowers are paler, or even white, and it was from one such variation that the Shirley poppies were developed. These have single, double or semi-double flowers in a wide range of colors, including yellow and orange. Both types of poppy have slender, bristly stems and narrow, lobed leaves.

WHERE TO PLANT
Field poppies are ideal for naturalizing in a wild meadow area within a garden or for growing in mixed beds in full sun. They can put up with poor soil and free-draining sand and chalk.

CARING FOR PLANTS
In late autumn sow seed of either field poppies or Shirley poppies where you want them to grow; seedlings are difficult to transplant. If you have chosen the right spot they will self-seed freely and form a natural colony year after year.

Shirley poppies thrive in poor soil and in meadow or praire-style plantings and come in a wide range of colors.

Persicaria bistorta

Bistort, snakeweed

ZONE 4–9

The densely packed spikes of small, pink flowers of bistort look best massed together in a great drift. It has strong "knotted" stems and elongated, grasslike leaves. Its common name, snakeweed, refers to its twisted roots.

The genus is a versatile one. As the name suggests, *P. amphibia* will grow in more than 12in (30cm) of water. *P. affinis* makes low-growing groundcover in sun or light shade. *P. campanulata* has fragrant, looser flowerheads arranged in clusters and does well in clay.

WHERE TO PLANT
P. bistorta is a plant of damp meadows and water margins, and it can be planted in similar situations within the garden. Use its upright flower stems, which can be to 2ft (60cm) or so, to add strong vertical lines to plantings beside ponds, in a mixed border with damp soil, or to brighten up the shade in an edge-of-woodland setting.

CARING FOR PLANTS
If bistort finds conditions too much to its liking, it can become invasive. When it threatens to overwhelm neighboring plants, divide and shift clumps in autumn or spring. You may prefer to remove spent flowerheads before they turn an unsightly brown.

Bistort is a fast-growing plant for damp meadows or for naturalizing beside a pond, lake, or stream.

110

Philadelphus 'Belle Etoile'

Mock orange

ZONE 5–9

Mock orange has simple, open flowers, well known for their sweet scent. The flowers of the cultivar 'Belle Etoile' have a contrasting purple blotch at the base of each petal. Cut flowering stems last well in water. The leaves often appear puckered because of their prominent veins.

WHERE TO PLANT
Because mock orange flowers in summer, it makes an ideal companion plant for tall shrub roses. It also makes a good addition to a mixed hedge. At an average 8ft (2.4m), 'Belle Etoile' is not quite as tall as the more widely grown species P. coronarius, which is more tolerant of dry soil as long as drainage is good. The cultivar P. coronarius 'Aureus' has greenish-gold leaves and prefers light shade.

CARING FOR PLANTS
Once bushes reach their full height the topmost branches can start to look bare and leggy. To avoid this happening or to remedy it, cut out about a quarter of the stems immediately after they have finished flowering. Repeat this year after year and you will keep the shrub neat and bushy. Aphids, especially blackfly, can be a problem.

The sweetly scented flowers of **Philadelphus** *'Belle Etoile' are distinguished by the dark purple blotches at the base of each petal.*

Phlomis fruticosa

Jerusalem sage

ZONE 4-10

In summer the subtle silver-gray foliage of Jerusalem sage is offset by whorls of two-lipped flowers in a refined shade of mustard yellow. The flowers are long-lasting, and after the petals fall, the seedheads are worth retaining for their interesting shape.

WHERE TO PLANT
Plant in a hot, dry spot in full sun and it will even thrive in drought conditions. Although they probably do best in free-draining chalk or sandy soils, they will still perform in clay.

CARING FOR PLANTS
If you grow Jerusalem sage in clay soil that may get waterlogged in a bad winter, there is a slight risk that you will lose the plant. Take some cuttings in autumn and overwinter them under glass as insurance. Cutting the whole bush back hard in spring rejuvenates the foliage, which can get a bit dusty-looking after a long hot summer, but will also delay flowering by a few weeks.

113

Jerusalem sage has two-lipped flowers that characterize plants from the mint family to which it belongs.

Pieris 'Forest Flame'

Pieris

ZONE
3–9

One of the main charms of pieris is its rich red new foliage in spring, which gradually fades to pink and finally a more prosaic green. When it flowers it has pretty sprays of white, bell-shaped blooms, but it does not always do this reliably. If you want flowers, *P. japonica*, the lily-of-the-valley bush, is the one you need, but it is not as reliably hardy in colder areas as 'Forest Flame' (also called 'Flame of the Forest').

WHERE TO PLANT
All species and cultivars of pieris must have acidic soil if they are to thrive. 'Forest Flame' will grow in full sun or in part shade and will tolerate a certain degree of dry soil—in a woodland area or below taller shrubs, for example. 'Forest Flame' can grow quite tall itself if you let it, sometimes topping 6ft (2m) after many years.

CARING FOR PLANTS
It's not unusual for the first flush of new leaves to be stricken by a late spring frost, but plants soon recover; the cultivar 'Forest Flame' is truly hardy. Wait until summer to cut back frost-damaged shoots. If you need to prune to reshape the plant, do this right after the shrub has flowered (if it does) or in early summer.

Pieris 'Forest Flame' is an evergreen shrub for acid soils, grown for its colorful new foliage in spring.

Potentilla fruticosa 'Elizabeth'

Cinquefoil

ZONE
5–9

Potentillas are compact, deciduous shrubs with a neat, rounded shape. They have a long flowering period, often from late spring to early autumn. *P. fruticosa* 'Elizabeth' is one of the easiest cultivars to grow. It has simple, primrose-yellow flowers. The leaves are tiny and glossy green and are arranged in groups of five.

WHERE TO GROW
Potentillas flourish in fairly poor but well-drained soil, as long as it doesn't get too waterlogged in winter. It is also worth trying them in clay soil. They flower most strongly in full sun but can put up with a little shade—for example, from a nearby tree in the afternoon. A row of shrubs makes a decorative low hedge about 3ft (1m) high.

CARING FOR PLANTS
Trim bushes lightly just after flowering and before winter. At the same time, cut out any dead stems or weak spindly growth.

Potentilla fruticosa 'Elizabeth' is a shrub that flowers for months on end, producing masses of simple primrose-yellow flowers.

115

Primula florindae

Giant cowslip

ZONE 6–9

Giant cowslip is native to the Himalayas and is suitably large. Its typical primrose-type leaves are extra long, forming a rosette to 3ft (1m) across from which it sends up strong stems topped with clusters of yellow flowers like the diminutive wild primula. The flowers are sweetly scented.

WHERE TO PLANT
Mimic giant cowslip's natural cool, streamside habitat by planting it in ground that never dries out—in a bog garden, for example, or in the margins of a pond. Provided the soil stays moist, the cowslip can put up with full sun, although shade is more to its liking. It also tolerates acidic soil (although it does not actually need it) and grows well in heavy clay. The flower stems may reach 4ft (1.2m), so do not plant it in front of anything too low or under a tree with low branches.

CARING FOR PLANTS
Leave flowers to set seed and you may be rewarded with self-set seedlings if conditions are right. Do not let plants dry out; if the soil does dry out, you have planted them in the wrong spot and had better move them.

The giant cowslip bears clusters of yellow flowers on sturdy, erect stems in summer.

Pulmonaria officinalis

Lungwort

ZONE 6–9

Lungwort has bristly leaves spotted with silvery white. In spring it produces sprays of small, drooping flowers that start off pink and fade to blue, giving a pretty two-color effect. Various cultivars have been developed, including 'Sissinghurst White' and 'Blue Mist'.

WHERE TO PLANT
Generally thought of as shade-loving plants, pulmonarias are ideal grown as groundcover in shady spots below shrubs and trees. Some cultivars, such as *P. officinalis* 'Sissinghurst White', also tolerate full sun, but they will not do as well in sun as in shade. As they are at their best in spring, do not give them too prominent a position in the garden because plants can look rather tired by midsummer.

CARING FOR PLANTS
Pulmonarias are prone to powdery mildew in dry weather. If plants become affected, cut the leaves right back to ground level and water well to encourage fresh new growth, which will ideally be disease-free. Plants often self-seed if you do not cut them back after flowering.

Lungwort is essentially a spring plant, when it produces sprays of pink and blue flowers above its silver-spotted leaves.

117

Rheum palmatum 'Atrosanguineum'

Chinese rhubarb

ZONE
6–10

The height of the flowering stems—8ft
(2.4m)—means that Chinese rhubarb makes
a big impact in a garden. Its flowers are fine
and feathery and reddish-pink in color and
look rather like dock. If you prefer not to
be reminded of a pernicious weed every
time you look at the plant, then cut off the
flowering stems (see Caring for Plants,
below). The leaves are deeply lobed and
hairy; those of the cultivar 'Atrosanguineum'
are purplish-red when young.

WHERE TO PLANT
Turn a bog garden into a feature with
Chinese rhubarb. You could plant one at the
edge of a large pond—it would dwarf a small
one—and it doesn't actually have to grow in
water, as long as the soil does not dry out at
any time of year. Mulching will help.

CARING FOR PLANTS
Removing flower stems before they get a
chance to bloom results in the plant putting
all its energies into producing even bigger
leaves. Plants appreciate a mulch of well-
rotted manure or garden compost in spring.

*Rheum palmatum 'Atrosanguineum' is a giant among
perennial plants and is closely related to culinary
rhubarb, as you will recognize if you have ever let the
latter go to seed to produce flower spikes like these.*

Rhododendron 'Loderi'

Rhododendron

pH ZONE 6–11

Rhododendrons are stunning spring shrubs and 'Loderi' has large fragrant flowers in trusses of ten blooms or more. It is quite a big variety at 6ft (1.8m), and in an average garden you will prefer one of the dwarf hybrids. 'Moerheim', for example, seldom exceeds 3ft (1m), has masses of violet flowers, is hardy and is one of the easiest to grow.

WHERE TO PLANT
Shade doesn't bother rhododendrons, which are largely woodland plants. What they must have without fail is acidic soil. Larger species make stunning hedges and useful windbreaks.

CARING FOR PLANTS
Deadhead shrubs to prolong flowering and improve appearance. In soil that veers toward neutral pH, add an annual mulch of pine needles to increase the acidity. Improve the drainage of acidic clay soils by digging in sand and well-rotted garden compost or leaf mold before planting. This will help their delicate, fibrous roots penetrate the soil much more easily.

The flowers of 'Loderi' are pink in bud but often open to white. A number of cultivars were developed from it in the early twentieth century, and all have 'Loderi' in their name.

119

Rodgersia pinnata

Rodgersia

ZONE
6–9

Rodgersias are grown for their beautiful architectural foliage. The leaves, to 3ft (1m) long, are tinged with bronze when they first appear, fading to dark green. Their bold shapes, coupled with their height, stand out against less well-defined foliage and give a border an almost tropical look. Plants do not always flower reliably, but when they do, they send up plumes of tiny, starry flowers in shades of pink, cream, or white.

WHERE TO PLANT

Water is the most important element. A bog garden is ideal, but rodgersias will grow in any naturally moist, water-retentive soil in sun or shade. Choose a sheltered spot protected from the coldest winds.

CARING FOR PLANTS

Do not let plants dry out. If the soil does not stay at least damp year-round, move the plant to a spot that does. Do this in spring or autumn, which are traditional planting times for many plants, including rodgersias. Dig in plenty of well-rotted manure or garden compost before planting and mulch regularly throughout the year to help keep the soil moist. Always mulch when the soil is wet.

Rodgersia doesn't necessarily flower every year, but many gardeners would admit to growing it for its graphic, well-defined foliage rather than its flowers.

Rosa rugosa

Sea tomato, Ramanas rose

ZONE
1–11

Rosa rugosa has simple, open, flat flowers of deepest pink with a central mass of yellow stamens. It is a very tough, vigorous, hardy rose, which stays in bloom from summer to autumn, after which it forms big, bold hips that are orange-red in color. Even the leaves contribute to the color scheme, turning golden-yellow before they drop. It is a prickly rose.

WHERE TO PLANT

Its dense, thorny habit makes it an ideal boundary hedge, shrugging off cold winds and heavy or salt-laden gales. Depending on conditions, it will grow to 4–8ft (1.2–2.4m) tall. Set plants out 18in (45cm) apart for an effective hedge or windbreak.

121

CARING FOR PLANTS

When growing *Rosa rugosa* as a hedge, prune plants hard in their first year. Clip and tidy up as necessary. Dig in plenty of well-rotted manure before planting and feed plants regularly.

Hybrids of Rosa rugosa have been developed that have almost fully double flowers, including the deep pink cultivar 'Hansa'.

Ruscus aculeatus

Butcher's broom

ZONE
7–11

The charms of butcher's broom are rather understated. It has tough, green leaves, which are actually flattened stems. In spring tiny, star-shaped, green flowers appear to sit on the surface of the "leaf." Male and female flowers are borne on separate plants, and if you grow both, the female plants produce scarlet berries. The real virtue of butcher's broom is that it grows in the most inhospitable, dry soil under shrubs and trees. Even if you haven't seen it growing before, you have probably come across it as a foliage plant in florist's bouquets.

WHERE TO PLANT
Grow butcher's broom in those shady "black spots," such as beneath evergreen trees, shrubs, or shallow-rooted trees like silver birch. Set plants out a couple of feet apart (60cm) and they'll make good groundcover. Butcher's broom will grow in sun, too.

CARING FOR PLANTS
Do not forget to plant a mix of male and female plants if you want a show of berries in autumn. Cut back any dead or straggly stems in spring.

An etching of frost adds the finishing touch to a clump of butcher's broom in full berry. Only female plants produce berries.

Santolina chamaecyparissus

Lavender cotton

ZONE
7–10

Lavender cotton is a low-growing, rounded bush with woolly white stems and finely divided, silver-gray leaves. In summer it has small, button-shaped, yellow flowers. Gardeners who grow lavender cotton for its silver foliage often trim off the flowerheads before they open, especially if the color would clash with a purple and pink border. The cultivar 'Lemon Queen' has gray-green rather than silver foliage and is taller and wider. 'Nana' is a smaller lavender cotton, suitable for a rock garden.

WHERE TO PLANT
The silver foliage is a planting clue: lavender cotton thrives in hot, sunny sites where the soil is free-draining or even positively dry. Use plants as a low dividing hedge, setting them out about 1ft (30cm) apart, between different plantings or set them alongside a path.

CARING FOR PLANTS
In fall, clip off old flowerheads and tidy up any overly long shoots. Cut older plants back hard each spring. Although lavender cotton is hardy, it's one of those plants that has a finite lifespan. After five or six years, bushes begin to look woody and leggy and are best replaced altogether.

The narrow, silver, greatly reduced foliage of lavender cotton is a classic adaptation to resist fierce sun and moisture loss.

123

Sarcococca confusa

Sweet box

ZONE 5–10

Best known for its fragrance at a bleak time of year, sweet box, also called Christmas boxwood, is a dense evergreen bush. It flowers from midwinter on, the clusters of small, creamy flowers contrasting with the glossy, black fruits from the previous year's blooms— that is if the birds haven't eaten the berries.

WHERE TO PLANT
Sweet box puts up with deep, dry shade. To make the most of its honey-scented flowers, position it where you will not have to walk far to find it on cold days. Plants eventually grow to around 6ft (2m) tall and 3ft (1m) across.

CARING FOR PLANTS
For best results, plants need shelter from the coldest winds; siting them near a wall or below taller shrubs and trees will help. Pruning shouldn't be necessary, except to reshape or to remove dead wood, which should be done in spring.

Winter-flowering plants are highly prized by gardeners, and this one, sweet box, also brings fragrance to cold dreary days.

Sedum spectabile

Showy stonecrop

ZONE 5–10

Late-flowering showy stonecrop brings a burst of color to the garden in autumn. The large, flat flowerheads are packed with tiny pink flowers. As soon as they open, they attract dozens of butterflies and bees. Even after the flowers have long faded, the dried stems and heads still look interesting, especially when etched with frost. The leaves are gray-greenish and thick and fleshy, and the whole plant overwinters as a densely packed mass of nubby buds. There are several cultivars, that differ mainly in flower color: 'Carmen' has crimson flowers, 'Brilliant' is a deep rose pink, and 'Iceberg' is white.

WHERE TO PLANT
The thick, fleshy leaves of showy stonecrop indicate its ability to conserve water in hot, dry conditions. Set it in full sun in free-draining soil. Waterlogged winter soils can cause the roots and whole plant to rot. Individual clumps seldom exceed 2ft (60cm) in either height or width.

CARING FOR PLANTS
Leave showy stonecrop's dead flower stems and leaves in place over winter, not just for their welcome textural effect but also to give a bit of extra protection to the developing buds below. In spring, old flowers and foliage should pull away quite easily, without any resistance.

The fleshy leaves of succulent, easy-to-grow Sedum spectabile are well adapted to conserve moisture.

124

Sempervivum tectorum

Hens-and-chicks, houseleek

ZONE 2–11

The bristly tipped leaves of hens-and-chicks are arranged in neat overlapping circles to form a rosette. Mainly blue-green, the leaves sometimes become flushed with color in summer and turn a subtle shade of red. At the same time, plants send up flowering stems topped with clusters of starry red flowers. The rosettes are low growing, typically 6in (15cm) high, but the flowering stems can reach 20in (50cm).

WHERE TO PLANT
Houseleeks can sometimes be found growing in old tiled roofs and garden walls. Their succulent leaves conserve water, and the way they overlap in a rosette also helps the leaves shade each other from the sun. Plant in full sun in the driest possible spot. They will rot in cold, wet winter soil.

CARING FOR PLANTS
An individual rosette that has flowered will die, but there should be plenty of offsets to make a display for years to come. Look out, too, for *S. ciliosum*, which has hairy leaves and yellow flowers and enjoys the same conditions.

The precisely overlapping leaves of Sempervivum tectorum *add form and texture to borders, pots, or containers in full sun.*

Skimmia japonica

Japanese skimmia

pH   ZONE 7–10

The sprays of pinkish-red flowerbuds make an attractive display all through autumn and winter before finally opening in spring. The flowers within are white and sweetly scented. Male and female flowers are carried on separate plants, and both sexes are needed for the female plants to bear bright red summer berries.

WHERE TO PLANT
Skimmia japonica grows in soil that ranges from acidic to neutral. Truly versatile, it does equally well in dry or damp soils, in sun or shade. Skimmias will grow in seaside and city gardens because of the marginally milder micro-climates. Plant among taller trees and shrubs for added protection against severe frosts.

CARING FOR PLANTS
Severe frost can damage new growth, which will turn white. Cut out any affected stems in late spring. Shrubs naturally form a rounded dome, ultimately around 5ft (1.5m) tall. The only pruning necessary is to take out any shoots that spoil the shape.

127

A female plant of Japanese skimmia bearing both berries and next year's flower buds. Female flowers will produce berries only if there is a male nearby.

Spartium junceum

Spanish broom

ZONE 6–11

The deep yellow flowers of Spanish broom are borne at the tips of the tough, dark green stems in summer and autumn. They are typical pea-shaped flowers and highly fragrant. Just like sweet peas, they are followed by pods, which are slightly flattened and dark brown when ripe. The leaves are tiny and sparsely scattered.

WHERE TO PLANT
As its almost non-existent leaves and tough wiry stems suggest, this plant is adapted to hot, dry sites. Cold soils that become easily waterlogged will kill plants quickly. Mix it in with other shrubs of a similar height—around 10 feet (3 m)—or set it against a hot, sunny wall where it can really bake.

CARING FOR PLANTS
To shape new shrubs, cut stems back to half their size in spring. Do this for three or four years until the plant has taken a good rounded shape. Thereafter, Spanish broom needs nothing more than a light trim in the spring. Never cut into old wood, as it will not regenerate.

Spanish broom is a useful plant for seaside gardens and often does well grown in containers on city rooftop patios.

Spiraea japonica 'Goldflame'

Japanese spirea

ZONE 5–8

Spiraea japonica is a late-flowering species with a range of cultivars. The leaves of the cultivar 'Goldflame' are a reddish-bronze when they first open, gradually turning yellow. The flowers are produced in flat heads, dense with tiny, dark pink, starry flowers. It is a low-growing shrub, making a compact bush about 3ft (1m) tall and across.

WHERE TO PLANT
S. japonica and its cultivars grow well in both clay and chalky soils. To make a low decorative hedge, set plants about 3ft (1m) apart.

CARING FOR PLANTS
Try not to let plants dry out completely, especially when they are young. Prune plants hard immediately after planting, to about 6in (15cm), and prune back to this size every spring for dense bushy growth. Deadhead the flowers as they finish.

129

Spiraea japonica 'Goldflame' flowers late in the year but in spring puts on a show of colored foliage that matures to yellow.

Stipa gigantea

Giant feather grass, needlegrass

| | | | ZONE 4-9 |

Giant feather grass forms a dense clump of dark leaves around 30in (75cm) tall. In summer, spectacular flowering stems shoot to 8ft (2.4m), bearing spikes of typical grassy flowers. The plant makes an impact all year, and only a heavy snowfall will finally see off old flower stems. These change color as they age, from golden to straw yellow, and when they get wet, they turn reddish-brown.

A scaled-down option for a smaller garden is S. tenuissima (Mexican feather grass, Texas needlegrass). It makes eye-catching groundcover and is extraordinarily mobile, moving gracefully in the slightest breeze. It will also self-seed.

WHERE TO PLANT
Grasses from the genus Stipa are native to prairies and wide open, dry grasslands. Set them in full sun in the driest part of the garden. They also do best in poor soil, because rich soil tends to encourage lax, floppy growth.

CARING FOR PLANTS
Cut out dead flower stems of S. gigantea in winter where practicable. Alternatively, shear right across the clump, but do not cut it right back to the ground in winter: wait until mid-spring before you carry out such drastic treatment.

Pull out spent stems of S. tenuissima in late winter.

Stipa gigantea is not a grass for small gardens. You need space to stand back and admire it, and appreciate how it moves in the breeze.

Syringa vulgaris

Lilac

| | | | | ZONE 1-9 |

Even though lilacs flower for such a short time, few gardeners grudge them space for their fragrant spring blooms. Those generally on sale are cultivars or hybrids of the common lilac, Syringa vulgaris, which has single purple flowers. From this lilac have been bred forms with flowers that are white, two-tone and shades of purple. For a small garden look for S. meyeri spontanea var. 'Palibin', which is much more of a shrub than a tree.

WHERE TO PLANT
Choose a spot that doesn't get waterlogged in winter and preferably in full sun or at least with minimal shading. Lilacs do not mind heavy clay or thin chalk and grow well in seaside gardens.

CARING FOR PLANTS
Cut off the dead flowerheads in early summer and pull off any suckers arising from the main stems. Overgrown shrubs can be cut back to about 3 feet (1 m) in winter. The vigorous new regrowth can be thinned and shaped.

Syringa vulgaris 'Charles Joly' flowers toward the end of spring and is highly scented. Its leaves are noticeably dark green.

131

Tamarix ramosissima (syn. T. pentandra)

Five-stamen tamarisk

ZONE
2–10

Tamarisk bushes are a familiar sight in many seaside towns, in public spaces, in gardens, and right on the sea walls where they are regularly drenched with spray at high tide. The overall impression they make is feathery, from the plumy sprays of pink flowers to the finely divided foliage. *Tamarix ramosissima* has pink flowers in late summer and autumn. It reaches about 20ft (6m) high. The other commonly grown species, *T. tetrandra*, is smaller—13ft (4m)—and flowers earlier.

WHERE TO PLANT
In exposed seaside gardens, tamarisk makes a useful shelter and a tough boundary hedge that is completely resilient to salt-laden gales. Sandy soils present no problem, and the bushes can withstand prolonged dry spells. They will not thrive in heavy clay soils that become waterlogged in winter.

Five-stamen tamarisk is banned as a noxious plant in Colorado, Montana, New Mexico, Nevada, Washington and Wyoming.

CARING FOR PLANTS
To thicken up bushes of *T. ramosissima* for a windbreak or hedge, prune them hard once they start growing in spring. Pruning also prevents plants from becoming top-heavy, precariously unstable; and susceptible to wind rock.

A tamarisk in full bloom is an explosion of pink plumes. Despite their delicate appearance they make tough seaside windbreaks.

Teucrium chamaedrys

Germander

ZONE
3–11

Germander has aromatic foliage, and its shiny, green leaves are thickly felted below with gray hairs. In summer it produces spikes of red, pink, white, or purple flowers.

WHERE TO PLANT
The facts that the foliage is scented and the undersides of the leaves are protected with hairs indicate that this is a plant for hot, dry sites and has adapted to a lack of water. Germanders are native Mediterranean plants and suit the same hot, dry conditions that lavender and other shrubby plants enjoy. *T. chamaedrys* grows to just 2ft (60cm) tall and so makes a good border edging, especially alongside a path.

CARING FOR PLANTS
Set out new plants in autumn or spring. Pruning shouldn't be necessary, unless you want to tidy up spent flowerheads after they have finished blooming.

133

For an aromatic treat crush the softly felted green leaves of Teucrium chamaedrys *as you pass by.*

Thymus vulgaris

Common thyme, garden thyme

ZONE
3–10

Thyme is a very well-known culinary herb, but it is also useful in the wider garden. Common thyme is quite variable in size and appearance: it may have pink or white flowers and can be anything between 6in (15cm) and 12in (30cm) tall. Plenty of other species work well in the garden, too, and nearly all are hardy. The principal requirement for all, however, is full sun.

WHERE TO PLANT
The tough, wiry stems, tiny leaves, and haze of aromatic fragrance mean that thyme can survive hot, dry sites in full sun. It's ideal among paving or stone slabs because these reflect the heat back to these sun-loving plants.

CARING FOR PLANTS
Set out new plants in spring or early summer to let them get established before winter. Inevitably, plants get straggly after four or five years, and it is easier to replace rather than try to rejuvenate them, especially as thyme roots easily from cuttings. A light clipping after flowering helps maintain vigor.

Thyme is tough enough to survive being walked on if planted between paving slabs, and releases its fragrance as it is crushed underfoot.

Tolmiea menziesii

Piggy-back plant

pH

ZONE
4–9

You might be more familiar with the piggy-back plant as a houseplant, but it does equally well outside, too. Its curiosity value is that it produces new plantlets on its leaves, at the point where the leaf joins the stalk—thus its common name. In spring and summer it has spikes of faintly perfumed, brownish, tubular flowers.

WHERE TO PLANT
Use the piggy-back plant as groundcover in dense or light shade. Keep it well away from direct sunlight, which will scorch the leaves, and plant it in moist soil. It is ideal for a woodland garden or for similarly dappled shade under deciduous shrubs and trees. It is perfectly at home in acidic soil though doesn't require it.

CARING FOR PLANTS
Carefully detach young plantlets from the parent leaf in summer and replant close by to increase groundcover. Be careful not to let plants dry out in hot summers or when they are still small.

The unusual brown flowers of the piggy-back plant make it a sophisticated choice for a damp shady border where the sun won't scorch its foliage.

134

Trollius europaeus

Globeflower

ZONE 5–9

Trollius europaeus is closely related to the buttercup and has typical deeply cut, buttercup-like leaves. In late spring and early summer it bears pale yellow flowers on upright stems. Several cultivars have been developed in a range of colors: *T.* x *cultorum* 'Alabaster' has creamy-white flowers; 'Orange Princess' has orange flowers; and 'Canary Bird' has lemon yellow flowers. 'Superbus' has enormous, 4in (10cm), sulfur-yellow blooms.

WHERE TO PLANT

Globeflowers do well along the edge of a stream, beside a pond, or in a damp ditch. They can also be grown in a border if the soil is moist enough; mulch around the plant to retain as much moisture as possible. They grow to about 2ft (60cm) tall and can cope with full sun or partial shade.

CARING FOR PLANTS

Cut back after flowering to encourage a second flush of flowers. If older clumps do not flower as prolifically, lift them in autumn and divide before replanting to give them more space.

Both the shape and color of the globeflower are clues that it is related to the common buttercup, but it prefers a wetter habitat.

Ulex europaeus

Gorse

pH · ZONE 6–9

This shrub, which is native to western and central Europe, has dark green stems, few leaves and vicious spines. It flowers first in spring and intermittently throughout the summer, with typical pealike, yellow flowers, which give off a delicious scent of honey on hot days. A mature shrub can reach 8 feet (2.4 m) tall.

WHERE TO PLANT

Its almost universal tolerance of difficult conditions makes it surprising that gorse isn't more widely planted, until you consider its extremely spiny nature. This means that gorse cannot really be grown as anything other than a windbreak or an effective, impenetrable property hedge. Plant it on awkward, dry, sunny banks or use it to shelter more delicate species in an exposed garden. Do not plant it close to paths, for obvious reasons.

Gorse is banned as a noxious plant in British Columbia, California, Hawaii, Oregon and Washington.

CARING FOR PLANTS

Tidy up gorse bushes after the first flush of flowers in spring. Occasionally, late frosts will scorch new shoots, but these can be easily trimmed back.

Gorse and Scotch broom (see Cytisus scoparius, page 70) share similar preferences for hot, dry habitats and both have yellow, pealike flowers.

136

Verbascum bombicyferum

Turkish mullein

With its great candelabra of intense yellow flowers, mullein makes a spectacular architectural plant. It grows to about 6 feet (2 m) tall, the flower stems rising up from a huge flat rosette of woolly silver leaves. Even the stems and bracts that encircle the flower buds are smothered in furry, white hairs. The cultivar 'Polarsummer' (sometimes referred to as 'Arctic Summer') is similar in size and appearance but has white flowers.

WHERE TO PLANT
With its heavily protected leaves and stems, mullein thrives in hot, dry sites. Its vast basal rosette of leaves offers useful protection from rain and sun on slopes and banks, helping to stabilize the soil surface. It puts up with a wide range of soils.

CARING FOR PLANTS
Mulleins often behave like biennials and die after flowering and are only short-lived as perennials, especially in hot, humid climates. None of which matters too much as they usually self-seed prolifically if conditions are right. You might need to stake the flower stems in a windy garden.

The dense, furry white hairs that cover stems and leaves are a good foil for the intense, almost sulfur-yellow flowers of Turkish mullein. The flowering stem produces many branches, creating a candelabra effect.

Viburnum tinus

Laurustinus, viburnum

ZONE 4–10

Whatever the time of year, there's always something to look at with laurustinus. The pink flower buds form from autumn onward and open over a long season from late winter to spring. The flowerheads are flat clusters of pinkish-white flowers. There are often flowers and blue-black berries on the bush at the same time. The leaves are dark green and shiny.

V. burkwoodii is another hardy evergreen viburnum that has scented flowers and downy brown undersides to its leaves. Other useful species include *V. sargentii*, which has red autumn berries; *V. plicatum* with its big, flat flowerheads that are rather like hydrangeas; and *V. farreri*, which has new bronze foliage turning to bright green as it matures. All three are deciduous.

WHERE TO PLANT

Try growing any of these species as a hedge, clipped formally or left to its natural spread. They are also good-looking enough to be a feature in a shrub border or by a garden entrance. None of these species minds full sun or light shade.

CARING FOR PLANTS

Trim hedges and prune formal hedges severely into shape after the main flowering in late spring. For specimen bushes, cut some of the older stems back to ground level to encourage new growth.

Viburnum tinus *'Eve Price' has a compact shape and habit. The flower buds tend to be more intensely pink than the flowers themselves, which are a paler shade.*

139

Vinca major 'Variegata'

Greater periwinkle

Periwinkle has long, questing shoots, that rapidly colonize bare earth. 'Variegata' has dark green, oval leaves edged with creamy white. The flowers are violet and produced intermittently throughout the year. It will scramble through taller plants or over low walls and fences. There are other periwinkles to look out for with different color flowers, which mainly belong to the closely related species, lesser periwinkle, *Vinca minor*. *V. minor* f. *alba* has white flowers; 'Burgundy' has magenta flowers.

WHERE TO PLANT
Periwinkle is useful for quickly covering a bare, shady bank, but plants may overstep their limits, so take care not to let them spread out of their allotted spaces. The denser the shade, the fewer flowers you will get, but the variegated leaves add interest. Periwinkle doesn't mind thin, chalky soils.

CARING FOR PLANTS
Cut plants back hard in spring to keep them under control. If you do not want periwinkle to spread any further, keep pulling back long shoots, which will root wherever they touch the ground.

Greater periwinkle flowers more prolifically in full sun but will still flower sporadically in shade. Cut back plants to keep them looking bushy.

ZONE 5–11

Yucca filamentosa

Adam's needle

The yucca plant's long, swordlike leaves can be up to 30in (75cm) long and sprout from a central rosette. In late summer these plants, which are native to the southeast states, send up tall flowering spikes, up to 6ft (2m) tall, packed with nodding flowers, like pendent inverted tulips, usually white with a hint of cream or green. The flowers last several weeks before fading. Look out for the cultivars 'Bright Edge', which has broad yellow margins to the leaves, and 'Variegata', with white edges.

WHERE TO PLANT

Make a feature of such a stunning specimen plant in a hot, dry spot or in a gravelly seaside garden. A yucca can look larger than life and dwarf any surrounding plants, so is probably best placed where it can be admired without distraction or where you need a vertical accent.

CARING FOR PLANTS

Cut down the flower stems when they have finished blooming. Plants in warmer areas should be fine over winter, but in frostier areas a winter mulch is wise, though Adam's needle is the hardiest of the yuccas and does quite well. Do not be fooled by its warm origins—desert nights can actually be very cold.

While the flowering stems of Adam's needle can top 6 ft (2 m), the actual plant seldom exceeds 3 ft (1 m) tall. The leaves of 'Variegata' are edged in white.

141

Index

Page numbers in *italics* refer to illustrations

143

Acknowledgments

Steven Wooster 1, 6 (top left), 2, 7 (right), 8-9 (John Brooke's Design), 11 (top left) (The Beth Chatto Gardens), 11 (top right) (Sticky Wicket, Dorset), 12 (Huntersville Station), 13 (Steve Wooster's garden), 14-15 (Jack Richards' garden, Wainui Beach, NZ), 17 (top) (Ram House), 18 (top) (Kilmokea, Ireland), 19 (top) ('The two Grahams' garden, Napier Region, NZ), 19 (bottom) (Butterstream), 20 (The Ellerslie Flower Show 1998, The Living Earth Company, Auckland, NZ), 21 (top) (Capel Manor), 26-27 (Clive Higgie's garden), 28 (left), 28 (right) (Hadspen Garden), 29, 30 (left), 30 (right), 31 (right), 32-33 (The Beth Chatto Gardens), 36 (top) (The Beth Chatto Gardens), 37 (The Beth Chatto Gardens), 39 (The Beth Chatto Gardens), 40-41 (The Folly, Picton, NZ), 45, 46, 47, 49, 50, 51, 52, 53, 56, 58, 60, 62, 65, 66, 67, 68, 69, 70, 71, 75, 76, 77, 78, 79, 81, 83, 88, 89, 90, 91, 92, 93, 94, 95, 97, 98, 101, 103 (Yalding Organic Gardens), 104, 105, 106, 107 (Suzette Gardens, Rakaia, NZ), 108, 109, 111, 112, 114, 115, 117, 118, 119, 120, 121, 122, 123, 124, 125, 126, 127, 128, 129, 131, 133, 134, 135, 136, 137, 139, 140, 141; **Collins & Brown** 4, 6 (bottom left), 11 (bottom) ('Gardening Basics'), 16 (left and right) ('Weekend Gardener'), 17 (bottom left and bottom right) ('Weekend Gardener'), 18 (bottom) ('Weekend Gardener'), 21 (bottom) (Howard Rice), 22 ('Weekend Gardener'), 23 (left and right) ('Weekend Gardener'), 24 (top, middle and bottom) ('Weekend Gardener'), 25 ('Weekend Gardener'), 31 (left), 34 (top, middle and bottom), 36 (bottom, all) ('Weekend Gardener'), 38 ('Weekend Gardener'), 43 (Howard Rice), 44, 48 (Howard Rice), 54, 55 (Howard Rice), 57 ('Plants for Free'), 59 ('Plants for Free'), 61, 63, 73, 74 ('Plants for Free'), 82, 84, 85 ('Plants for Free'), 87 (Howard Rice), 96, 99, 100, 110, 113 (Howard Rice), 130 (Howard Rice), 132 (Howard Rice); © **J. S. Sira/Garden Picture Library** 64; © **Howard Rice/Garden Picture Library** 72; © **John Glover/Garden Picture Library** 80; © **Sunniva Harte/Garden Picture Library** 86; © **Jerry Pavia/Garden Picture Library** 102; © **Christi Carter/Garden Picture Library** 116; Unless otherwise credited, all other photograpy was taken by Steven Wooster; *Front cover (top left):* Brachyglottis (photo: Steven Wooster, pg 52); *Front cover (top right):* Echinops ritro (photo: Steven Wooster, pg 75); *Front cover (bottom left):* Lonicera sempervirens (photo: Steven Wooster/Yalding Organic Gardens, pg 103); *Front cover (bottom right):* Sempervivum (photo: Steven Wooster, pg 126); *Back cover (left):* Enkianthus (photo: Steven Wooster, pg 77); *Back cover (middle):* Kniphofia (photo: Steven Wooster, pg 97); *Back cover (right):* Nepeta (photo: Steven Wooster/Suzette Gardens, Rakaia, NZ, pg 107).

A Zone Map of the U.S. and Canada

A plant's winter hardiness is critical in deciding whether it is suitable for your garden. The map below divides the United States and Canada into 11 climactic zones based on average minimum temperatures, as compiled by the U.S. Department of Agriculture. Find your zone and check the zone information in the plant directory to help you choose the plants most likely to flourish in your climate.

below -50°F	Zone 1	Below -45°C
-50° to -40°F	Zone 2	-45° to -40°C
-40° to -30°F	Zone 3	-40° to -34° C
-30° to -20°F	Zone 4	-34° to -29° C
-20° to -10°F	Zone 5	-29° to -23° C
-10° to 0°F	Zone 6	-23° to -18°C
0° to 10°F	Zone 7	-18° to -12°C
10° to 20°F	Zone 8	-12° to -6°C
20° to 30°F	Zone 9	-6° to -1°C
30° to 40°F	Zone 10	-1° to 5°C
above 40°F	Zone 11	above 5°C